"I was born on April 29, 1937, in Trier, Germany during the dictatorship of Adolf Hitler. The following story is an account of my survival during that time and represents a perspective that often goes unnoticed in our world's history. It's a perspective that's shared by millions of Germans who were powerless to stop Hitler and his regime from the horrific acts of violence they perpetrated against all German citizens, both Jewish and non-Jewish alike." — Elisabeth B. Couture

Copyright © 2015 by Elisabeth B. Couture

All rights reserved, including the right to reproduce this book or portions thereof in any form whatsoever.

Thanks to Daniel Meader for his creative writing.

Special thanks to Brian Couture for his writing contributions, editing and cover design.

Edited by: Courtney Lindemann

Printed by: CreateSpace

Front Cover Photo: (Pictured left to right.)
Back Row: Berta Louise Lentes (Pregnant with Guenter.) and Jakob Lentes.
Front Row: Elisabeth Berta, Wilhelmine, Ewald, Eduard, and Matthias.

Berta's Beginnings

by Elisabeth B. Couture

Chapters

1	Final Embrace	1
2	Gunshot Shattered	3
3	Apocalyptic Roar	10
4	Journey Back	23
5	Momma's Strength	26
6	What Gretel Did	44
7	First Strike	48
8	Clinging to the Shadows	60
9	The Man Grabbed Berta	66
10	Reassuring Hand	69
11	Father's Permission	73
12	Next Phase	82
13	Days at the Orphanage	85
14	Gasping for Breath	90
15	Eating for Two	101
16	Out for Thirty Days	109
17	Something was Different	118
18	Leaving for America	133
19	New Orders	138
20	Dream Come True	145
21	Elisabeth's Beauty Salon	150

Final Embrace

    Sawdust, the type of which her father carried home each day—stuck to his jacket, coating his boots, peppering itself through his hair and brow—now fell on Berta's head as she clung to his leg. She didn't understand why he was leaving them. Berta wondered...had she done something to make him unhappy? The mind of a child racing, crafting simple solutions, reeling to grasp at the answers to a problem born by means too complex for even the grown mind to unravel.

    Looking down on the top of his daughter's curly head, Berta's father remembered the spring that she was born—a time of year when everything was shiny and new—his infant girl fitting right in. And now, surrounded by his family, he remembered the handful of years before the war started. Living their lives, what worries they had striking him as minor in comparison to what they now faced. With his daughter still attached, staunchly refusing to release her grasp on his leg, the man shook hands with his eldest sons and kissed his eldest daughter on the top of her head. Sandwiching Berta between them, he shared a final embrace with his wife. Wiping her eyes with the back of her hand, Mama peeled Berta away from her father's leg. The proud man placed a hand on top of his little girl's head, afraid to linger, lest his emotions get the best of him.

Avoiding the reality of the war for years, it had finally come to take its toll on the family—as it would many others in the coming months. Unsure if he was saying goodbye to his family for the last time, the man turned back briefly at the door, flashing a smile he hoped was reassuring. With that, he left, leaving his family standing together, wondering what would come next.

Gunshot Shattered

Neighbors gathered in the front yard on an unseasonably warm afternoon. Tired and agitated, the town women found a rare opportunity to greet one another and socialize; laughter punctuated the hum of their chatter as children flitted around their legs. Swatting hands dissuaded the tugging of skirts; rare smiles breaking across faces that had lately been creased with worry. Two older boys chased their younger sisters around the ruffled hems of their mother's dress.

The boys soon tired of playing with the smaller children, and Berta, the youngest of the five, wandered off to play with the neighbor girl, Anna. They shared the same dark, curly hair and birthdays in the spring. Skipping a small stone across the cobbles, they kept rhythm with songs—melodies garbled by infectious laughter. Lost in their game, the heavy footfalls did not register until well after they had already rounded the street corner. The men approached from behind—dressed neatly in black from helmet to steel toed boot. They enveloped the girls as they marched by, stirring curly heads in the wake of their passing. Mouths agape, eyes wide, Berta and Anna looked

Elisabeth B. Couture

as if they were trapped in a photograph where the action was occurring just outside the frame. Heavy boots kicked down the front door of Anna's house.

    Calloused hands pulled an ashen faced man across the threshold; fingers clawed at the door frame as his frail body was forced into the sunlight. The gray wisps of his hair were nearly invisible against the white stone wall of the family home. Either cowering in fear or stooping from his many years, the man stood huddled, outlined against the stone. His glassy eyes reflected the darkness of the uniforms in front of him. The expression on his face not one of pride, nor defeat, but of fear.

    The soldier in charge took two large strides away from the old man and turned as he drew a well worn pistol from the strap at his waist. Extending the weapon at shoulder height, he froze the man with a glance. The soft cry that hung in the silence could have come from the mouth of the old man or the two young girls, standing helpless. In either case it was quickly swallowed by the heavy report of the pistol.

Berta's Beginnings

The gunshot shattered through heavy air trapping the girls; leaving them motionless. Berta quickly jumped backwards as her heart and her throat met. Her eyes reflected the sudden color of the wall as the old man fell. Clutching at great handfuls of air, she searched for Anna's hand at her side. Latching on, Anna was slowly led toward the relative safety of Berta's house just as the soldiers' barking was intersected by the scream of the woman crouched over the man's body. A half dozen steps from the front gate, Berta placed a hand on the door knob just as it swung open, her mother quickly ushering both girls inside. Berta's siblings watched from the bedroom.

"Let go Berta," her mother yelped as she grabbed Anna's upper arm and shuttled her to the closet. Shoving boxes aside, Mama propped open the door to the crawl space beneath the house. Lifting the girl under the arms, she lowered her into the darkness, raising a finger to her lips to signal silence.

Berta shook her hand, damp with sweat, before wiping it across the front of her dress. Catching Anna's eye as the cellar door was lowered and the boxes shifted into place, Berta thought that she might never see her friend again. She shuddered. Her mother moved quickly to her side and whisked her into the bedroom where her brothers and sisters sat, dumbfounded, staring at her. Berta sat on the edge of the bed and listened to her mother stalk the kitchen. Getting the nerve to wander out, she looked up at her mother, who ceased her pacing.

"Why is Anna hiding?"

"Her family is Jewish Berta; Anna is Jewish." Only daring a tentative nod, Berta watched her mother turn towards the window. For the first time that day she was just as scared as she was confused.

A lady came to the door that night. Berta with swollen eyes, eavesdropped from her bed as the lady spoke with her mother. The crawl space door opened and closed with a creak, unsettling the normal night time sounds of the house. Berta was never to see her friend again.

Berta's Beginnings

As morning broke the next day, the children's bedroom was silent despite the five children it contained. The echo of boots on cobbles snapped everyone's attention to the window. Men drifted in and out in droves, sweeping out the young and able bodied. Cries were drowned and tears diluted in the swirling of coats, boots, and heavy breath—crashing and receding until it was one great noise.

Rough hands reached from tan coats: smashing doors, shedding the grasp of wailing mothers and snatching wide eyed children from their homes. The cries were unbearable. The joy of gathering in the front yard long evaporated; the women a numbing siren, a klaxon for mercy.

The framed picture of the Führer peeked out from its resting place behind porcelain that Berta was not allowed to touch. Mama flew to the china cabinet, snatching it from his perch in response to the atonal rhythm of foot falls in the street. She retrieved the photograph from its place and hung it on the lonely nail above the door. She kept the nature of madness from her children for as long as possible. As a buffer from the noise, ten strong hands pressed against five sets of small ears.

Berta snapped her head around as the door cracked twice before exploding inward, splintering into a deformed mouth. Four German soldiers scrambled into the small home, forcing her mother aside and locking hands around the flailing arms and writhing legs of her three older siblings. Berta caught her brother Ed's eyes as he was dragged from the room. A glazed look returned her stare, reflecting nothing. The soldiers removed Thias, Minchen, and Ed from their childhood home. It all seemed unreal.

The cacophony receded almost as suddenly as it had begun. Berta looked on as her mother deflated to a heap of wrinkled fabric on the kitchen floor; her husband taken from her months before, likely lost to the horrors of war. Children she had fought to shield from the outside world—the world that just came crashing through her front door—now lost to her as well.

Berta's Beginnings

Berta crept among the dust and debris of the kitchen floor to her mother's side. She knew her mother was strong but she didn't know how to respond to the defeated figure before her. Crouching down and burying her face in her mother's chest, Berta clung as tightly as she could. Mama clutched her daughter to her, placing one hand on her back and another on her growing belly. She knew that she would have to keep herself together—for herself and her children: Ewald, Berta, and the child she carried.

Elisabeth B. Couture

Apocalyptic Roar

As it turned out, the new year wore two faces: An infant's innocent cries fell from one mouth while another stretched grotesquely with the howl of war. With her father and older siblings gone, Berta, five years removed from infancy herself, was left to help her mother with baby Guenter.

Every Tuesday and Thursday Berta, her brother Ewald, and baby Guenter squirming in her arms, would peek through the window as the horses pulled a cart of food and clothing down the street. She stood on tip toes while Mama ran out to greet the cart, returning with arms full. At nightfall, lamps were darkened and the windows draped with black fabric from the rations cart.

The house, lit by candlelight and without so much as the glow of the moon, took on a somber mood in the evenings. Unknowing and brazen, Berta brushed the heavy curtains with her hand, knowing her mother was out of the room. Hooking a foot around a table corner, Berta lurched forward, wrapping her small fist in the window covering as she sprawled to the floor. Startled by the commotion,

Mama flew into the room, incensed by the scene. Ignoring Berta's cries, she quickly re-covered the window before turning sternly to reprimand her daughter. Yanking Berta to her feet and gripping her shoulders, the woman's voice pitched several octaves above her normal speaking voice.

"Berta! What were you thinking? You never think!" She snapped as she shook the girl firmly. Recognizing that it was fear, and not anger, in her mother's voice, Berta finished her sobbing. Sniffling, she looked into Mama's tired eyes as her face relaxed into a comforting half smile.

"Mama..." Berta all but whispered. "It's to keep you safe liebchen; no more playing near the curtains, understand?" Berta did not understand, but she did as she was told and gave the windows a wide berth going forward. Everything was starting to scare her.

Sirens wailed, announcing the arrival of American planes. The room spun as Berta sat up, rubbing her heavy eyes. The fever was worse, sheets damp with sweat. She had spent the day in bed and was unaware of the hour.

A particularly whiny air raid alarm pitched its warning from close by, letting everyone know to take shelter in the musty smelling bunker up the street.

Punctuating the din, rusty hinges groaned as Mama flung open the bedroom door. Brushing her hand against Berta's forehead, she pursed her lips until they formed a thin white line. Moving in a blur, Mama whisked her from her soggy sheets and across the hall to the bathroom. Berta, eyes full of sleep and head lolling from side to side, barely kept her balance as her arms were raised and the small night gown was tugged loose over her head. Semi-conscious, she felt her feet leave the ground as Mama dropped her into a tub of ice water. With shock breaking the haze of sleep and fever, Berta's scream created a dissonant tone to the warning alarms still ringing out.

Blue lipped, she sat shivering—left to take inventory of the limbs she could still feel as her mother scuttled to the bedroom to shush the baby. Berta's fingers became tiny prunes. Once more Mama rushed in, pressing her impossibly warm hand to Berta's forehead.

Berta did not know if the fever had broken or if Mama had just decided that they could wait no longer, but as she was lifted from the tub all she felt was grateful to be rid of the frigid water. Roughly dried and hastily bundled, Mama—with mewling infant clutched to her chest—hurried Berta to the door. Struggling to keep pace on short legs, Berta gasped at air that felt as though the ice water from the tub had filled her chest. Frozen hair matted to her face, she wound one hand in her mother's long dress, using the other to tap out the seconds between distant explosions, like spring thunder.

"Keep your eyes down; the shining wire is death!" cried the man on the corner of the next street. The whites of his eyes were in stark contrast against his soot covered face. His hand clutched a tiny shoe.

"Berta, close to me." Mama said, as Berta clutched tighter to her side.

Rounding the street corner, the family noticed that the bunker doors stood open as neighbors filed inside. Berta raised her hand to point out the bunker, looking up towards her mother for assurance. They got within a hundred yards.

The ground rang as if a great bell had been struck; the homes around them lit up like noon time on a clear summer's day. Mama dropped to the ground on top of her children as the noise swallowed them.

Berta was sure, that it was the most terrible sound she had ever heard. Her next thought was wondering if it had even made a sound at all. It was a feeling; a wave that surrounded her and pulled her under. The winter air melted and began to boil. Berta tried to cough fire from her lungs.

Debris rained down around them. The fieldstone bunker was decimated. The homes of people they knew stood naked, ripped apart.

Mama covered them for a long time. Cowering... shaking... Berta pressed her face to the stone and her hands to her ears. Sound returned all at once: her baby brother Guenter's sobbing hiccups, women screaming, wounded cries, sirens ringing for eternity. Berta pressed the sides of her head until her arms shook.

Mama rose to her feet pulling the children with her. Women streamed passed them towards the flaming bunker to begin the frantic search for friends, neighbors, and family. Berta approached the rubble, still attached to her mother's side. They, too, began to dig. The alarm was finally put to rest, and it was only the voices that remained. Berta shifted warm stones from the pile. The sunrise found them still digging.

After clearing the bunker, it didn't take long for the SS (Hitler's personal guard.) to arrive, going from house to house and barking orders. Berta knew they would have to leave. Mama packed little: clothes, some pictures.

"We're taking a train to see the mountains." she

offered Berta, feigning excitement.

They were transported to the small resort town of Bad Bertrich, where they would be sheltered in hotels. Protected by treaty, the town would be home to women, children, and wounded soldiers from all sides.

Never having been on a train, Berta was wary, but interested. Her town was not the same as it once was. She saw only sad faces on the street. Meeting neighbors on the walk to the train station, she felt as though they were people she hardly knew.

The train was crowded. Stale breath hung in the air, and Berta saw the world as a roiling sea of restless legs and clumsy arms swinging heavy luggage. Clutching her mother's hand, she put her back to a corner. The air was musty, desperate eyes searched nervously, there were no windows. Berta slouched against the wall and fell asleep with her head on her knees. Her mother's sturdy legs in front of her, she felt safe tucked into her corner.

Berta's Beginnings

A disembodied voice jolted her awake as it blared from the corners of the crowded car. Wiping sleep from her eyes, Berta tried to make out the words over the heightened chatter of fellow passengers. Looking nervously up at her mother's face, she could tell that the news was not good. As everyone quieted to listen, she locked eyes with Mama as the message to evacuate the slowing train crystallized over the crowd.

The lull in energy erupted into an all out frenzy as the train lurched to a halt. Yanking Berta's arm nearly from its socket and lifting her a good foot into the air, Mama began the fight towards the door. Berta felt the air escape from her lungs as the weight of the crowd pressed in on her, crushing her against her mother's hip. A man's wool jacket, like sandpaper, pressed to her cheek as the crowd surged and struggled.

Managing to squirm towards the door, they emerged to a foggy mid-morning. Wasting no time, Mama guided her children to the tree line. Holding the baby tight, she forced them all to the ground once more. The brush crunched softly underneath them, sticky and wet. Berta remembered the bunker, she burrowed under her mother, hands on her ears.

The drone of airplanes in the distance multiplied into an apocalyptic roar as they passed overhead, firing on the train. Lead peppered the ground, showering everyone in dirt and mud. Trees popped and exploded, dropping limbs on top of bodies huddled to the earth. Berta could hear Mama humming loudly—an attempt at distraction. Catching only snippets through ringing ears, Berta gritted her teeth to the point she thought they may shatter.

The chaos eventually wore itself out. Those that remained pulled themselves from the dirt and congregated around what was left of the train. Berta padded back into the train wearing only socks—her shoes lost in the mud. She watched the shafts of light play across the carriage floor, filtering through new holes in the cabin. Faces she failed to recognize before were all the more indecipherable in their masks of dirt and blood. As damaged as the train was, everyone was able to re-board and continue on their journey, eventually arriving at the hotel.

At the hotel, they were given a small room on the third floor. One bed for the four of them. Mama spent her days working down in the laundry room or preparing meals. The children were confined to the room—a fast moving brook just outside the doors proving to be too much of a danger. They lived in close quarters and were left wondering what the war might bring as they spent much of the year cooped up.

An elderly man, leaning like a fence post, hobbled down the street with a stained brass bell each day, shouting the latest news of the war in a voice stranger than one would expect from his diminutive frame. An overcast afternoon in September saw the man barreled down the narrow street; the speed of youth reuniting with his old legs and the dusky sky matching his pallor despite the flush of his cheeks. He hollered as loud as ever—Berta catching snippets from her place on the floor, occupying the baby.

"Russian soldiers... red from the windows!" Mama found an old red blouse. Using some twine she strung it from the window of the room. Peaking out from around her mother as she worked, Berta saw that nearly everyone in town had done the same. Mismatched, impromptu flags whipped from every window as a breeze whistled through the street.

Twenty minutes later, the man shambled back into the square, having lost some of his pep. Now urging everyone to replace their red with white, as it was the Americans who would be marching into town. The sheet was torn from the bed. Mama retrieved her blouse and replaced it with the sheet. It looked as though everyone had elected to dry their laundry at once.

Shortly thereafter, Mama gathered the baby and goaded Berta and Ewald downstairs. The majority of the town lined the streets, craning their necks for a view of the American troops. Berta held her mother's hand and wondered what it might be that could have everyone so eager. Mama wore a look of apprehension, knowing that it was the Americans who were responsible for the attack on their train a year prior. She kept her chin up and her children close.

The Americans marched by in rows of four. As the soldiers approached, Berta couldn't help but notice their skin. She had never seen anything like it. Their eyes shown out from dark faces. White teeth brighter than she had ever seen. Even in the daylight, they seemed to glow. One soldier came to a halt directly in front of Berta, dropping to a knee. His eyes were red, tired, and a little sad. He licked his lips before he spoke.

"Candy?" he asked, opening his outstretched palm. Berta recognized the chocolate in the center of his pink palm. She stole a glance up at Mama who only seemed to glower back at her. The soldier unwrapped the bar and took a small bite. "Mmm," he encouraged and smiling as he chewed—lips pulled back, glowing teeth smudged with cocoa. Berta's stomach growled. Looking up at Mama once more, her eyes pleading for approval. She was rewarded with a curt nod. Quickly snatching the bar from the man's hand, she devoured it in three large bites. It had been so long since she had tasted candy. Her eyes thanked the man, who placed a large hand on her head as he rose to his feet and continued his march down the street.

The next day, there was an aggressive knocking at the door. Mama opened it to reveal two American soldiers. The soldiers rudely entered the room, grunting unintelligibly and rifling through everything they could get their hands on. One soldier began to tear through pictures that had made the long journey from home. Mama cried out, but was restrained as a large man spoke loudly to her in a language she did not understand. After they left, three more soldiers arrived in short order, this time with a German translator. He explained that the American soldiers needed the hotel and that everyone would have to leave. Packing the few remaining things she owned, Mama once again prepared to depart.

Journey Back

The war was over. There were no trains to take the displaced back to their homes. Mama traded a farmer one of her dresses for a small wooden cart, pulling it along with the baby sleeping soundly inside and Berta trailed behind. To what home they were returning, she did not know.

Nothing was as they had left it. The promise of home that had sustained them on their journey back had evaporated at the site of what was once their neighborhood. They had returned to ruins. Debris was scattered everywhere. Lives replaced with piles of rubble. Everything was scorched—blackened and shattered beyond repair. They happened upon their house, where nothing stood but a second story toilet—suspended in the air, independent of everything that had once stood around it.

The public pool house was the last structure on the block left standing. Mama led them there as a last ditch effort to put a roof over their heads for the foreseeable future. The roof was leaking; Berta thought it smelled like feet and gutter water. She kicked pebbles into the pool and watched the murky water swallow them, oily ripples slithering outward.

Mama made a home for them in the pool house as best she could. They had no idea how long they would need to stay. With the war over, they were now left to fend for themselves—the rations carts could no longer be relied upon. Food was scarce, to say the least. Berta was left to scavenge for anything even mildly edible. Neighbors gave the little they had to offer.

Berta padded over the dusty cobbles; her shoes frayed from the long walk home. Hunger gnawing at her, she placed her hands over her empty stomach. A hunk of dry bread, picked clean of the bits of mold invading its edges, was all the four of them had eaten since the evening before. Noticing a trash can outside a recently reoccupied house on the corner, she swallowed her pride and approached the bin. Leftovers and scraps proved to be enough to quiet the rumble of her stomach. She collected what she could in a small bag, darting back to the pool hall to show Mama.

Families were slowly sent off to new homes. Mama came to the morbid realization that in many cases, "new" meant the abandoned homes of their Jewish neighbors. However, those grim thoughts were all but forgotten with the news that they had been assigned a new home of their very own. Mama said a quick prayer for those that had been lost, bundling her children and the last of their belongings before departing for "home."

Elisabeth B. Couture

Momma's Strength

The new house was bigger than Berta expected. After the close quarters of the small hotel room, and the miserable week at the pool house, she was in heaven. Enjoying the fresh air, and the feeling of home, she plodded through the garden. Weeds grew taller than her head in the untended soil.

"Oh mein Gott!" A cry from the front yard got Berta's attention. She raced to the front of the house, paying no mind to the mud churned up by her shoes that speckled the back of her dress. Breathing heavily, wide-eyed with surprise, Berta found Mama weeping and clutching the two children that had just been returned to her. Berta rushed to greet them; her brother Ed lifting her by the underarms as Minchen looked on smiling through her naturally sad eyes.

"Inside, inside with all of you!" Mama cried, not attempting to hide the relief in her voice. She cleared her throat through the tears, failing to mask the undeniable excitement she felt.

A long day of getting reacquainted had sapped Berta

of her energy. Laying in bed, she listened as her mother spoke to her older siblings in the den.

"They brought Thias and I to the same camp. We were split up as soon as we arrived." Ed spoke in clipped sentences, as if afraid to say more than he had to. "I never saw him again."

Unable to parse the hushed whisper produced by her older sister, Minchen, Berta could not keep up with the story of her time away. What she could hear was sobbing and the sounds of Mama comforting her gently. Berta could hear the soft tap of Ed's shoes as he paced uncomfortably across the wooden floors. She fell asleep, her mind unable to comprehend what they had been through. It was not something she wanted to consider.

The following weeks were not what Berta had in mind when she imagined reuniting with her lost siblings. The sores on her ankles itched something terrible. It felt as if her ankles were covered in burning insect bites. Under strict orders from Mama not to scratch, Berta could do little but paw at the restlessly aching wounds on her lower legs. Staring up at the afternoon sun, she silently cursed Minchen for bringing this disease into the home. Beads of sweat wound their way down her brow, matting down the thick curls. Minchen said she saw many of the girls with whom she was held come down with the very same symptoms. Mama added that Minchen may have been a carrier for the illness, even if she never had it herself. Banished to the old wooden yard chair by Mama—in hopes that the sun would solve the problem—Berta did nothing but sit and wait. Legs too weak to hold her, she was carried to and from the chair by Ed as days crept by.

The gate groaned open, startling Berta out of her daydreams. Fighting through the sun blindness, she struggled to identify the intruder. Silhouetted against the afternoon glare, stood an older man, steering a well used bicycle with one hand. His dark hair was slick and greasy. Shirtless, his skin was tan and oily with sweat. Sitting bolt upright, Berta was speechless. The man approached, wearing only a pair of worn swim trunks; a pair of girl's shoes swung from his narrow shoulders. Crouching with his hands on his knees just a few feet from Berta, he opened his mouth to speak:

"Ber-Ta" he drew the word into two long syllables with a wide grin.

Confused as to how this stranger knew her name, Berta recoiled. The splinters of the chair pricked her back as she slid to the edge of the chair, plotting out the best course of escape.

"Do you know who I am?" the man continued. Noting the look of unease on the young girls face, he assumed she did not recognize him. "Berta, it's me. Your father." The man opened his arms, leaning in towards her.

Thinking that it must be a fever induced hallucination or a deranged stranger, Berta took in a lungful of air and screamed with everything she had. Mama nearly took down the front door as she barreled into the yard. Stumbling to a clumsy stop, Mama clutched both hands to her heart and began to weep. Finding her legs once more, she ran to the man and threw herself into his lean arms. Berta looked on, completely lost, as the man tucked his face to the crook of Mama's neck and began to laugh.

The last Berta had known, her father had been locked in a Russian prison camp. Still stuck in a state of paralysis, Berta's eyes turned to the door as her siblings rushed out to greet the man. Berta held baby Guenter in her arms, leaning in with her teary eyes as the man planted fat kisses on both of her cheeks. Ed clasped the man's hand, receiving a tousling of the hair and a firm pat on the back.

Breaking away from the picture of a happy family, the man approached Berta once more. Taking a knee beside her, he slung the shoes from his shoulder and offered them to Berta.

"For me?" Berta questioned meekly as she began to realize that this strange, nearly naked, man might be her father after all.

Berta's Beginnings

"Specially for you Bertie." as he so affectionately called her, grinning ear-to-ear; the man embraced her.

Berta began to cry and hugged the man tight. She liked the smell of him. It made her feel safe and, for a moment, she forgot about her itchy legs. Pulling away, but still grasping her shoulders with his outstretched arms, Papa gave her a wink as he stood up and turned back to Mama. Everyone, except Berta, returned to the house. Berta, in a state of shock, absently whacked at her swollen ankles.

Just as Berta was beginning to wonder if her family had forgotten her, Papa breezed by her with a wry smile. She watched curiously as he swung through the front gate carrying a small bucket. Losing sight of him, she glanced back to the front door to see if Mama would follow.

A few minutes later Papa returned, balancing a full bucket with one hand. Berta watched as he scooped a handful of thick, black liquid from the pail, cupping it in his palm. Grabbing Berta's leg with his free hand, Papa began to slather the goop onto her ankle. First one and then the other. Berta disliked the strong smell, but the syrupy stuff was warm on her bare legs.

"A little hot tar will knock it right out Bertie." Her father muttered, as he finished covering the inflamed skin.

Papa took over the duties of carrying Berta back and forth to her chair. The application of the warm tar became a daily ritual until Berta's legs began to look significantly better. Healed enough to walk, Berta could not believe that she had ever doubted this man. She thought that everything was nearly perfect. The only thing missing was her eldest brother, Thias.

Standing at the gate, Mama's hand on her shoulder, Berta watched her father depart once again on his bicycle. Although disappointed to see him leave, there wasn't any fear around his journey this time; he was going to search for Thias. After only a few days away, Berta was surprised to hear her father's voice again so soon. Skipping into the kitchen to greet him, she was dismayed to see that he was alone. They sat down for dinner feeling somber.

It took Papa two more tries before he tracked down his son in Bavaria, Southern Germany. Once home, the boy was not as Berta remembered him. He was moody, quick to anger and a look of distrust always seemed to cloud his once friendly face. Thias fought with Papa constantly. Berta was not surprised the next morning when Mama told her that he had run off in the middle of the night.

Papa retrieved him once more and, this time, he stayed for good. Although still irritable around Papa, the boy Thias was before the war began to reappear when in the company of his siblings. Berta started to notice the old twinkle in his eye. The familiar feeling of home returned to Berta again.

Berta wondered how she had ever doubted her father upon his return. She took to standing in front of the mirror wearing her biggest smile, letting her fingers linger over the creases and dimples that proved beyond a doubt that she was her father's daughter.

Berta had grown used to this question, knowing it was Papa's way of pestering Mama into finding a new place to make their own; a place where the air didn't hang so heavy with the memory of those who had come before.

There was a year where everything seemed to settle. The new house gave everyone some much needed space. Berta shared a room with her sister and the boys bunked in the adjacent room. Papa turned his attention to resurrecting his lumber business.

Over a series of weeks, Berta looked on as her Papa hovered over the boys—instructing them on the finer points of vehicle maintenance. Abandoned military vehicles had become commonplace. Broken down trucks were left to rust of the sides of recently retired supply routes. It wasn't long before the young men had an old truck growling back to life. Berta learned to identify the truck's unique rumble—the windows gently rattling in their frames as Papa returned from delivering a hefty load of wood.

Money being useless as it was after the fighting,

everything the family needed was acquired through Papa's bartering with neighboring farmers and families: Milk, eggs, meat, even a particularly inquisitive pig were all obtained by trade. Papa knew where to find wood suitable for furniture, as well as the kind needed for heating homes—both vital to building a new life.

Sunday mornings became particularly special. Berta longed for the weekly expeditions. Papa would lead the children into the woods. Light filtering through the heavy foliage and Papa's sun dappled face wavered in and out of shadows as he pointed out the various berries, nuts and mushrooms that were safe to eat. He always spent extra time showing his children the details of the particularly nasty, non-edible varieties. It was during times like these that Berta loved her father the very most. Hanging onto every word, she would try to remember each bit so she could demonstrate this knowledge in the future, hopeful to impress her father.

Still chattering with excitement from their morning with Papa, the children rushed back home with stories for Mama. Stern faced, urging the children to wash up and sit down for Sunday lunch—yet unable to resist Papa's good mood—Mama fought back a smile as Papa danced her around the table. Papa offered Mama a sly wink, a pat on the bottom, and an exuberant "Let's eat!"

A year later, Mama grew sick. She began complaining of headaches. As she grew more and more ill, the doctors began to suspect that it might be something more serious. Medicine was scarce and the medicine for what was finally diagnosed as meningitis was rarer still.

The hospital was nothing more than white walls, white sheets, and brass bed frames with chipped white paint. Berta heard the hiss, crackle, and spit of the radiator against the far wall and noticed that, it too, was white. A wave of disinfectant stung Berta's nose as she wandered timidly amongst the rows of beds. She tried to consider the smell they were attempting to mask and promptly stopped considering. Mama was in the third bed from the back, on the right side of the room. Thias gave Berta's hand an extra squeeze as they approached Mama's bed.

Her eyes rolled over to meet her children. Set deep in dark sockets and blinking slowly, paper thin eyelids revealed delicate blue veins. Her pallor matched the décor around her. Berta felt the tears well up in her eyes. She reached out to grasp a trembling hand. Mama's strength had left her, unable to reassure her daughter with a firm grip.

"How are you feeling Mama?" Thias muttered, voice cracking, trying to hide his uneasiness from Berta.

Mama's only response was a look of confusion through glassy eyes. All sense of recognition having left her.

"Mama..." Berta's voice quivering. Parting her lips to speak through a parched mouth, all Mama could manage were soft clicks and whispers. Berta stood silent as Thias ventured off to find a nurse, returning with a small glass of water. Tipping it to his mother's mouth, liquid dribbled down the corners of her face and onto her white hospital gown. Struggling to speak, Mama could manage nothing more than a brief series of humming and the faint "la, la" sound of her tongue against the roof of her mouth.

Thias—able to understand a great deal more of the situation than Berta—wandered off to the hallway, not wanting to break down in front of his sister. He watched Berta from the doorway as she spoke to their mother. Berta chattered away; Thias wondered what it was she was saying to their unresponsive mother.

The Sunday afternoon breeze carried the sound of church bells through the kitchen window. Food on the table, the children getting settled in to eat. Papa remained standing—head hung, face pale. Raising his head revealed new lines and creases that Berta had not noticed before. He looked older.

"Your mother passed away this morning." It was as if a great glass dome had been placed over the house and its inhabitants. Any sound from the outside world sealed out; the family sealed in—their heavy breath recirculating endlessly. Berta tapped her fingers nervously against the underside of the table. Thias cleared his throat repeatedly. For a short time, at least, it didn't seem real...nothing did. Papa sat down. They ate in silence, each lost in their own little world of shock and disbelief.

After lunch, the family began their personal procession down the street to the church where Mama's body was being kept. Greeted by a stern faced nun, Papa explained who they were and why they were there.

"I'm sorry for your loss," the nun offered, sounding sincere but practiced in her condolences. "Unfortunately, the body has already begun preparations for the service. I'm so sorry, but I cannot allow you to see her."

Papa couldn't manage to coax an argument from his mouth—words stuck in his throat, producing a humming kind of cough. He turned from the nun to the waiting faces of his children; the last of the color drained from his face.

The funeral procession was one of the largest the town had seen in quite some time. Mama's penchant for sharing what she could, even when the family could ill afford it, was reciprocated on that day. Papa felt silly for all the times he had pestered her for giving away a loaf of bread as he was greeted by the sullen faces of what seemed to be the entire town, come to pay their respects and mourn for the woman who had gone out of her way to help so many.

The last of the funeral crowd trickled out of the house. Berta thought it strange that Thias was seeing the last of the well-wishers to the door instead of Papa. She thought maybe he had gone to lay down but as the night went on, darkness fell with no sign of Papa. Thias assured her that he would locate their father before Berta put herself to bed.

When she woke in the morning, her brothers were gone and still no Papa. Berta and her sister made a light lunch with what they had on hand as they waited for the boys to return. The sun signaled later afternoon by the time the boys returned. Their Papa was still nowhere to be seen.

Days went on like that, with the boys heading out early and coming home just before dinner empty handed. It took about a week of this daily ritual before they turned back up with a man who at least vaguely resembled Papa. His eyes were streaked with soot, lips cracked and bleeding. Greasy hair poked out at strange angles and was recently—if not currently—drunk. Berta could smell him from across the room. His bloodshot eyes fell on her as she stood, clutching the door frame. With a look of shame, he quickly glanced away, wiping his hands nervously on his soiled clothes before briefly resting his hand on her shoulder. He opened his mouth to speak, but quickly closed it. Berta thought that his breath smelled like gasoline.

"Go to bed Berta," Thias muttered brusquely as he hustled Papa to the bathroom to clean him off.

Berta did as she was told. She was glad to have her Papa back, but worried if he would be the same man after all.

Struggling as he was to adjust, Berta found it hard

to connect with her Papa. Even when they were in the same room she felt as if he was someplace else, perhaps somewhere with Mama, if only in his head. The lumber business was a distant memory, and one he did not seem too likely to recall. The brothers sought work elsewhere. Life was very different at home. Berta's sister, having taken ill, was collected by her godmother to receive treatment. On the day she was to leave, Papa sat looking sullen and unaware.

"Goodbye Papa," she offered. Papa looked up, nodded and directed his blank stare back out the window. The brothers being at work, Berta was the only one left to see her off. Latching to her legs and squeezing tightly, she received a sweet kiss on the top of her head before her sister was led off.

Early one afternoon, a few weeks later, there was a knock on the front door. Papa, still hardly recognizable to Berta, was the first to answer. As he swung the door back he was greeted by a short, squat woman. Despite Papa's grizzled visage, the woman was strangely cheerful in his presence. She set forth with her widest smile and extended her hand as she explained who she was and why she was there.

"Good afternoon sir," she chirped "My name is Caroline and I'm a social worker from the local orphanage, just down the street. I've come to offer my condolences, as I've learned about the recent passing of your wife—"

"You can either get off of my front step right now, or I can throw you off. Those are your only two options!" Papa bellowed in the poor lady's face. Taken aback, she took two shuffling steps backward and tripped off the ledge of the stoop. Collecting her balance she gathered herself, huffing and puffing as she went, waddled back down the street from the direction in which she came.

Berta did not know if she was more surprised by the wanton disregard her Papa showed the woman, or by the fact that it was the most emotion that she had seen from the man in a long while. Slamming the front door, Papa marched—with unsure footing—back down the hall to his bedroom, rattling the door shut behind him.

Elisabeth B. Couture

What Gretel Did

Papa was drunk more and more often now. Berta could smell it on his breath as he brushed passed her at home. He sat slumped in his chair, mouth agape, alcohol sweating from his pores. In his presence her steps grew softer and her words whispered.

Arriving home from school in the afternoon, Berta was confronted with an unusual scene in the front room of her house. Her eldest brother already being out of the house and her sister gone away to live with an aunt, the room was filled with the remainder of her family. Her second eldest brother, Ed, leaned against the sink by the far wall, smoldering. She caught his eye for a moment as he quickly averted his gaze to his restlessly shifting shoes. Her father stood, leaning against the table next to a strange woman. Stringy, black hair hung limp at her shoulders. As she looked up at Berta's entrance, the light from the still open door revealed eyes like a puddle formed below a gutter after a spring storm—still reflecting the remains of the passing cloud front and rippling with each new drop of rain water. In her arms she held Guenter absently, as if she were ready to drop him at a moment's notice if presented with a better opportunity. Berta felt the hair on the back of her neck stand up, electrified, as the woman's lips folded back to reveal yellow teeth. It was as if a character from a deranged bestiary had wrapped her brother in its grasp—an animal threatening at every moment to shirk any sign of perceived domestication.

"Sit, Berta." her father choked out, clearing phlegm from his throat. "This is Gretel. She is an old friend. I was engaged to her before I met your mother. She will be staying with us now; make her feel welcome."

At this, Berta's brother Ed cleared his own throat and shuffled silently out of the room. Berta had no way of knowing at the time that he would be gone from their lives within a matter of months—his departure brought on by a set of circumstances headed by this strange new woman. Rising from her chair, Berta approached the woman and offered to take the baby. To this Gretel obliged with careless immediacy, causing Berta to act quickly lest her little brother hit the floor.

School for Berta began eight in the morning and was dismissed at two in the afternoon, six days a week. Upon her return in the afternoon, Gretel made sure that Berta's chores were waiting for her. It was as if Gretel waited for Berta's arrival every day, lingering by the door wearing an identical sneer, eagerly shoving a broom into her hand. Berta began to wonder what Gretel did all day long if she was expected to care for the house upon her return from school each afternoon. Berta would get to work cooking, cleaning, and seeing to the needs of her little brother. Exhausted by the end of the day, she still had her studies to attend to. Refusing to let Gretel impede on her dream of finishing school, Berta curled up under the covers with her flashlight to complete her homework.

On one afternoon in particular, Berta arrived home from school just in time to see her brother, Ed, storming out the front door. Gretel ensconced in the same chair as on the day Papa first brought her to the house. This time, she was not holding little Guenter but still wore the same vicious grin.

"Where is Ed going?" Berta questioned. Gretel, still as a gargoyle, held Berta in her gaze.

"I've gotten rid of him first. I'll get rid of as many of you as I can, and then it will be just your father and I."

Feeling a sudden cold wash over her, Berta hurried through the room, watching the woman from the corner of her eye to assure herself that she wasn't about to lunge at her, fangs bared. Gretel's head turned on her strangely elongated neck as Berta breezed passed, but she did not peel herself from her perch.

First Strike

Berta dreamed of becoming a hair dresser once her schooling was complete. The dream seemed to be slipping from her grasp as Gretel made her life more and more difficult. When Berta brought up her plans for the future to her Papa, he always had the same response: "After graduation you will find a job as a live in maid and learn how to run a household properly, before all else!"

Little did he realize that Berta was essentially running the house by herself already, simultaneously dealing with school and Gretel's relentless harping.

Years went by that way. Berta carried on as best she could, careful not to allow Gretel the satisfaction of breaking her down over time. Berta felt more and more estranged from her Papa the closer he grew to Gretel, until, finally, she lost all understanding of the man she thought he was.

The door flew open, shaking the entire room as it collided with the wall. Berta's head snapped towards the noise as her body went rigid, hunched over the desk in her bedroom. Her Papa's face had melted into a mask of rage. He swiped one hand over his sweat slicked face as the other quickly worked at loosening his belt. He managed to release the clasp with one hand and unfastened the belt in a single swift motion—the leather tip dusting the floor as he hung it menacingly at his side. He approached Berta and yanked her desk chair back one handed. Berta fought to catch her balance, but soon found her Papa's hand on the nape of her neck, forcing her off her seat and onto the floor. Adrenaline and disbelief kept her body from recognizing the initial blow, however the subsequent strikes broke through her stunned resistance. Berta cowered as blow after blow fell around her shoulders, back and legs. Just as suddenly as it had began, the onslaught ceased. Papa stood above her, panting for breath.

"I told you to show Gretel respect. Do not make me tell you again." Papa grumbled, his breathing returning to normal. "She told me what you said to her when she brought me my lunch this afternoon."

Berta did not know what to say. She clung to the

floor with her hands over her head, shaking and crying. She hadn't said anything to anger Gretel and she had no idea what Gretel could have possibly told her Papa to make him react this way. Deciding that silence was her best course of action, Berta's mouth remained sealed. Her Papa's footsteps receded down the hallway, the front door clicking open and rattling shut. Peeling herself from the floor, Berta wiped her face with her dress and brushed away the dirt. As Berta turned to face the hallway which her father had departed, she saw Gretel silhouetted in the doorway. On her face was carved the same smile Berta had despised from the day they had met.

The change that came over Gretel's face whenever there was a knock on the door became so commonplace to Berta that she hardly noticed it anymore. It was as if Gretel expected bad news each and every time they had a visitor. On one particular afternoon, the reason for her skittishness became abundantly evident.

On this afternoon, Berta opened the door to reveal a skinny, dark haired girl looming over her. Beside the strange girl was a set of three-year-old twins, two older girls and a boy about eight years old.

"Pardon me, but is there a Gretel Wuertz living here?" The girl spoke in a strange cadence, situated halfway between a whisper and a cough. Berta thought it odd that she had never before heard Gretel's last name spoken aloud.

"Yes, she does live here. Please, would you come in—" but before Berta could finish her sentence and open the door wide enough to let the six kids inside, Gretel swooped in, shoving Berta roughly aside.

"I told you never to come looking for me," Gretel shrieked, at a pitch sure to start every dog in the neighborhood barking. "Now go right back where you came from!"

At this, Gretel reared back and slammed the door in the faces of all six children. Dumbfounded, Berta stood back in silence, having just witnessed a new low for Gretel—

something she would not previously have thought possible.

As soon as Gretel had moved to the bedroom she shared with Berta's father, presumably to recover from the confrontation, Berta took off out the front door and sprinted all the way to her Papa's work. The thought of her Papa's anger when she told him of Gretel's response to the strange visitors quickened her pace. When she arrived, she found her Papa standing out front of the building where he worked, almost as if he were expecting her.

"Papa!" Berta gasped, not even waiting to catch her breath. "You'll never guess who just came to our house."

"What are you doing at my work, Berta?" Papa grumbled, his displeasure evident. As Berta told him what had transpired at home, his attitude turned from one of mild annoyance to moderate surprise. "Is that all Berta? Go back home and don't bother me at work again." He turned on his heel and disappeared back into the building.

Berta stood in stunned silence. She fought to decide

whether she was more horrified by Gretel's despicable actions or by her Papa's lack of any noticeable emotional response. Her feet dragged through the dirt on the route home. All of the energy sapped from her body.

The day after the unexpected visit—from whom Berta could only imagine to be Gretel's abandoned children—Berta arrived at the house to find her Papa home early from work. He was slumped in a kitchen chair, refusing to lift his head to meet Gretel's eyes across the table.

"Good afternoon," Berta muttered as she slunk past them, towards her bedroom. After placing her bag on the floor, she ventured to the adjoining bedroom to check on her younger brother. Surprisingly, she found Guenter's bed empty. He was nowhere to be found. With mounting worry, Berta searched the rest of the room to find that some of his clothes were missing. Berta's heart jumped into her throat. Flying down the hall and back into the kitchen, Berta slapped the table with the palms of her small hands.

"Where is he," Berta yelped. "What have you done

with Guenter?" Her father did not rouse at all, continuing to stare absently at the table top. "Papa, where is he?" Her father's silence was louder to her than her own voice, even though it cracked with the strain of increased volume and the tears choking the back of her throat. Finally, she turned to Gretel. "What...what have you done with him?" Gretel turned her cold gaze on Berta.

"Didn't I warn you that I would get rid of as many of you as I could? Did I not tell you that? I am a woman of my word little Berta."

"Where is he you WITCH?" Berta spewed the word towards Gretel's face like a barbed weapon. No sooner had it come out of her mouth, Berta's head snapped to the side and her cheek, burned as if it had been pressed to the stove top. Gretel struck her so hard and fast across the face that each individual finger stood out in crimson on Berta's cheek. Berta's father sat, as if nothing had happened at all, as if he sat in the room alone.

Berta flew to her bedroom and slammed the door.

Berta's Beginnings

Burying her face in her pillow, she let loose a reticent scream into the downy fluff. She screamed until her ears popped, then laid face down, gasping for breath. Berta later found out that Gretel had sold Guenter to a farmer; she thought she would never see him again.

    Morning came the next day, Berta waited until her Papa left for work before she emerged from her bedroom. As much as she hated Gretel, she wanted to see her Papa even less. Crossing the threshold into the kitchen, out of the corner of her eye, Berta spotted Gretel sitting in the same chair as always. Perhaps she was some kind of gargoyle; maybe she didn't sleep, but instead sat plastered to the chair throughout the evening. Collecting herself, Berta passed by without uttering a single word or even giving Gretel a glance. Instead, she began to put away the dishes that had been left on the rack to dry overnight. Berta could feel eyes boring into her back. The physical sensation of Gretel's eyes on her skin made the hairs on her neck stand and the flesh of her arms crawl.

    Out of nowhere, Gretel shattered the silence

between them.

"You're nothing but a little tramp, just like your mother." Disdain dripped from each syllable that fell from her wretched mouth. Berta did not turn around and did nothing to acknowledge what Gretel had said. Inwardly, however, the rage fueled Berta like a furnace. She could feel the blood rush all the way to the tips of her ears, her entire face flushed. Mentally, she tried to devise a way to get out of the kitchen without her reddened face adding to Gretel's satisfaction. Placing the last of the dishes in the cupboard, Berta turned around and walked out of the kitchen with her head down. As she passed by Gretel, she heard a lilting chuckle gurgle up from her throat.

The final insult being Gretel's laughter, something inside of Berta snapped. She glided soundlessly into the room that Mama and Papa used to share, dragging a hand along the bedspread under which Papa now spent his nights with Gretel. Careful to avoid the creaking floorboards that would give away her position, Berta approached the wardrobe and carefully opened the doors.

Berta's Beginnings

Her Papa's winter coat was slipped from its weighted hanger and laid across the bed. Berta then unhitched the hanger from the rod and hefted its substantial weight in her hand. Closing the wardrobe doors, she trusted her feet to carry her, as she could no longer feel any part of her body. The rage consumed her, narrowing her vision to only that which was immediately in front of her. Turning the corner and prowling down the hall, her pace quickened as she reached the kitchen. Sure enough, Gretel was just where Berta had left her, smoking a cigarette nonchalantly.

The first strike from the hanger knocked the glowing cherry from the end of her cigarette, causing it to topple onto Gretel's blouse instantly producing an ugly singe mark. Berta watched as the welt across Gretel's face raised itself immediately; almost as quickly as Gretel raised her hands to her face in self-defense. Berta relented momentarily before resuming with a volley of brutal strikes. Gretel fell to the floor screeching inconsolably as her hands, head, arms, and torso received the bulk of the impact. Bloody knuckles quivered against her face as another blow opened a gash on her forearm, sprinkling blood across Berta's blouse. The rod snapped from the bottom of the hanger causing Berta to quickly readjust her grip to compensate. She now struck with the top half and hook of the hanger. Anger had numbed her arm, allowing her to evade fatigue. It was as if she had become a simple machine whose sole purpose was to wildly swing the bloody hanger she gripped in her hand.

Suddenly, Berta felt a strong hand grasp her wrist. She looked up into the face of her brother Ed. Fortuitously for Gretel, he had just happened to be stopping by the house to check on his little sister. Equally as lucky for Berta that it was not her Papa, as she had feared upon feeling the strong grip. Berta dropped the hanger and began to cry, burying her face in her brother's chest. Gretel lay bloody and whimpering, looking very much the worse for wear. Ed stepped over Gretel and dragged Berta to her bedroom.

"Pack your things, quickly. If Papa gets his hands on you, he'll kill you." Ed took two quick strides to the closet and threw a small suitcase down on the bed. Berta did as she was told and packed all the essentials she could fit into the diminutive case. Her hands shook as she fought to latch the clasps.

"Let's go, now. Take my hand." Berta placed her shaking hand into her brother's steady one and let him lead her back through the hallway, passed Gretel's now nearly motionless body which splayed across the kitchen floor, and out the front door. She looked quickly back over her shoulder and wondered if she'd ever see her house again.

Clinging to the Shadows

They walked for such a long time that eventually the anger that had warmed Berta wore off as she became very much aware of the chill. Late afternoon had turned to night, and Berta watched the tops of the trees swaying in silhouette against the moonlight. They walked down what seemed like a never ending road. Ed walked ahead; Berta lagged behind. Her small suitcase—thumped rhythmically against the side of her knee. She caught herself absentmindedly timing her breathing pattern to the thump of the suitcase—two thumps...breathe in, two thumps...breathe out.

Around what must have been—to Berta's best guess—close to midnight, they arrived at the river. It first revealed itself as a glimmering reflection of the moon between the trees. Soon they were close enough that Berta could make out the street lamps bracketing the bridge. Also visible were a handful of men patrolling the bridge, close enough that Berta could see the breath slipping from their mouths in gentle clouds.

"On the other side of that bridge is Luxembourg," Ed

whispered, visibly straining to keep his teeth from chattering together. "We'll have to cross underneath in order to avoid the guards. It's shallow just below the bridge, but your shoes may get a little wet. You'll want to take your socks off first in case you have to spend the night out doors. You'll appreciate having something dry to slip over your feet."

Berta did as she was told. They sat together by the roadside and removed their socks, damp enough as they were from the sweat of their feet. Pulling their shoes back on over bare feet they approached the bridge. Ducking off the road just before it crested up to the bridge entrance, they scuttled down the embankment to the water below. Ed carefully picked his way down, offering a hand to his sister at the bottom.

Clinging to the shadows on the underside of the bridge, the pair made their way across the river and into Luxembourg. Keeping to the darker side of the street until they were out of sight from the guards, Ed led Berta into a dark and quiet park.

"I'm going to have to leave you here Berta. I need to get back before daybreak." Berta could hear the regret shrouding Ed's voice and understood that he couldn't stay with her. She was going to be on her own now, and she'd have to get used to that. Before departing he found her a bench and removed his jacket to give her an extra layer of warmth for the night.

"Won't you get cold on the walk back?" Berta questioned.

"I'll be fine Bertie, you just stay safe and try to stay warm. Put those dry socks back on now. I told you that you'd be grateful to have something warm on your feet." Ed managed to crack a sad smile as he hugged Berta close. "Stay warm tonight and in the morning knock on every door on this street. Someone could surely use the help of a live in maid. That will give you some place to stay for the time being and a little money in your pocket. We'll see each other again."

With that he slipped out of the park, and Berta lost

him in the shadow of the bridge. She strained her eyes to see a small silhouette wading back across the river and up the embankment on the opposite side.

Sitting on the bench and removing her shoes to put socks back on her pruny feet, Berta was immediately thankful for the tip. Clutching her brother's jacket tightly, she laid out across the bench, using her suitcase to prop her head up. She lay awake until dawn listening to the sound of the nearby river and the rustling of the park at night.

Early the next morning, Berta rose from the bench and ventured into town to begin knocking on doors. Luckily, it didn't take more than a dozen houses before Berta found someone who was receptive to her inquiry.

"Come in darling." said the kind-faced, elderly woman of the house. Berta gratefully obliged, feeling instantly thankful for the warmth inside the small home. Looking her up and down, the woman spoke, "A live in maid you say?"

"Yes ma'am," Berta responded.

"Well then, I can't say as I need much help around here, it being such a small house. I'm more able then I look young lady," she spoke with a wry smile. Berta thought she may have to knock on a few more doors yet. "But…" the woman continued "I do have a brother who owns a small nursery. He is always looking for more help. Let me give him a quick call and we'll see if he might be able to help you out."

"Thank you so much ma'am, I would love that!" Berta sputtered excitedly.

"Okay, one second dear. Take your coat off and make yourself at home."

The woman left the room, leaving Berta to sit on the couch alone and hope. At the very least, Berta thought she would get the chance to warm herself up before returning outdoors. Mere moments later, the woman returned with a smile on her face. Berta rose from her seat expectantly.

"I've spoken with my brother and sure enough he could use an extra pair of hands for planting this season. If you're interested, he's agreed to provide you with room and board in exchange for your assistance. How does that sound to you?"

"That sounds excellent ma'am. I'm grateful for the opportunity!" Berta failed to hide her excitement and relief, but she could tell that the woman appreciated it just the same.

"However, he won't be able to make his way down to pick you up for a couple of days yet, so I hope you don't mind staying with me for a couple of nights."

"I'm pleased that you'd have me ma'am," Berta spoke through a wide smile. Berta stayed comfortably with the old woman for two nights. She was fed well and was even given a real bed in the guest bedroom, as the woman lived alone. In two days time the woman's brother stopped by in his truck. Berta said goodbye to the kind old woman and hopped into the passenger seat with her suitcase in her lap.

Elisabeth B. Couture

The Man Grabbed Berta

Days at the nursery started at four o'clock every morning. Berta had a small room to herself and would rise early, wash and step into the green house in the dark hours before dawn. She often found herself alone, working in the humid room with only the plants as company. She didn't mind the solitude and grew to enjoy the smell of the soil. It was still late winter, and there was not too much for her to do until spring.

A month or so slipped by, and Berta began to grow comfortable in her role. She almost never saw the lady of the house because her room was so secluded. Though she spent most of her time in the greenhouse, it was rare that she spent much time talking to its proprietor. He had deliveries to make and would only stop in to make sure she was doing things correctly and not neglecting her duties.

Even as winter slipped into spring, the mornings were very cold. Having spent the end of winter in the relative warmth of the greenhouse, Berta now had to begin the task of transferring the seedlings to where they would be planted outside. Though the frost had broken, the cold dew still sparkled on the plants outside in the early morning. Try as she might to chase the cold from her hands, nothing Berta did to warm them was successful. No matter how vigorously she rubbed them together, Berta could not regain enough feeling to properly handle the seedlings and planting tools.

"How is everything coming along out there?" the man who owned the nursery inquired, poking his head out from the greenhouse door.

"My hands are having a hard time with the cold," Berta responded. "Do you happen to have a pair of gloves that I could borrow?" The man waved Berta into the greenhouse. As she stepped inside, she immediately felt uncomfortable with the way the man was looking at her. She couldn't quite put her finger on what it was that she was bothered by. Perhaps the look in his eye or his vacant smile.

"Come over here dear, and I'll show you how to warm up your hands." The man grabbed Berta by the wrists and dragged her towards him. Berta could feel his sickly sweet breath against her face. Surely, she was smelling whatever he had for breakfast that morning. Still grasping her by the wrists, the man attempted to force both of her hands down the front of his pants.

Berta reeled back in horror, kicking at the man, struggling to loosen his grasp. She let out a piercing scream, which seemed to jolt the man into releasing his hold. Perhaps, she thought, he was afraid of having to explain the noise to his wife who sat just inside the house.

The man turned and went back to examining his plants as Berta tore out of the greenhouse. As fast as her legs could carry her she ran back up to her room, packed what little she had back into her luggage, and rushed to the front door. Bursting out the front door, Berta looked back over her shoulder repeatedly, convinced that the man would be following her the very next time she looked. No one followed, but Berta continued to run down the street, tears streaming down her face.

Reassuring Hand

Having hitched a ride with a kind stranger, Berta found herself back in town. In fact, she found herself back at the very same bench on which she had spent the night months prior. Dropping her suitcase to the ground, Berta slumped onto the bench and wept with her hands covering her face. She was right back where she started: with no money in her pockets and no roof over her head. Hopelessness engulfed her, and she sobbed until she felt like she'd run out of tears.

Lifting her head from her hands and wiping her eyes with the sleeves of her coat, Berta noticed that she was no longer alone on the park bench. A statuesque woman, wearing the habit of a nun, sat stoically beside her. Berta wondered how long the woman had been there watching her cry. Speechless, Berta stared into the woman's kind face; eyes puffy and cheeks red. A feeling of embarrassment swept over her.

"I'm sorry sister." Berta choked out.

"You have nothing at all to be sorry about my dear,"

the nun crooned. "I am, however, curious as to what has gotten you so upset."

Berta, grateful to have someone to talk to, blurted out the story of the morning's events. As she spoke, she grew nervous that she might offend the nun with the crassness of the tale. There was no need to worry, at the end of the story the nun simply gave a curt nod and placed a reassuring hand on Berta's shoulder.

"If it is a job and a place to stay that you need, my dear, then I think that I may have just the place. You see, I live and work in a seminary. Do you know what that is?" Berta nodded to signify that she followed what the nun was saying. "We cook and clean for the young men studying for the priesthood. If you would like to join us, we could always use the help of a nice young girl such as yourself."

"Thank you sister," Berta gasped. "That sounds wonderful." She did not know if it was appropriate to hug a nun, so instead she gave her the most genuine smile she could muster. Together they rose from the bench, and Berta followed as the kind nun led the way.

Upon arriving at the convent, Berta was led directly upstairs to a small room that she was to have all to herself. The nun instructed her to make herself at home and to meet back downstairs in the common area once she had gotten settled. Berta was overjoyed. She unpacked her small suitcase, placing the few items she had in the small dresser next to the bed. The room was sparse, but it was hers, and it would keep her out of the cold. More importantly, it would keep her safe from the likes of the man at the nursery.

Having settled in as best she could, Berta descended the steps back down to the first floor to find the nun waiting for her calmly in a high backed chair.

Sitting opposite the nun, Berta folded her hands on her lap and straightened her posture. Over the course of the brief, but informative conversation, it was explained to Berta that she would have one day free every week to do as she pleased. During the week she would help with the chores. Cooking, cleaning, looking after the needs of the young priests. Anything that was asked of her by the older nuns, she would be expected to comply with. The nun told her that when she was finished with the days chores, she was free to sit in on lessons with the other sisters. Sewing, crocheting, knitting—there were many opportunities that Berta could pursue in order to benefit herself in her downtime. Berta was overjoyed, and knew that she had finally found a place that she belonged.

Father's Permission

Berta stayed with the nuns for three years. It had become her home, and she wanted nothing more than to become a nun and make it her life. She sought the council of the nun who had found her on the park bench three years ago. Berta had grown to trust this woman above all others. Sitting down one afternoon, Berta revealed her wish to become a nun.

"This is excellent news," the nun responded, showering Berta in the glow of her smile. "However, since you're only seventeen, you'll first need to get your father's permission. Berta's heart sunk. She had heard that both her Papa's brother and sister had joined the seminary, and was hopeful that fact would aid her in gaining her Papa's permission. The two had still not spoken, or even seen each other since Berta had left home. Berta assured the nun that she would do her best to acquire her Papa's permission. She was determined to do whatever it took.

Berta went right back up to her room and began to pen her Papa a letter:

Dear Papa,

I know we have not spoken in quite a long time, and for that I am sorry. The past three years of my life have been spent living in a small convent in Luxembourg. I have loved my time here and wish to join the seminary on a more permanent basis. One of the nuns here has informed me that, due to the fact that I am still only seventeen and not quite an adult, I will need to acquire your written permission to stay here. I do hope you will understand. I wish that this letter finds you well.

Berta

Berta's Beginnings

On the bottom of the letter Berta wrote the address of the seminary in hopes that her father would return a letter with his signature of consent. She mailed the letter and hoped, as that was all that she could do.

The very next Sunday one of the sisters came upstairs to tell Berta that she had a visitor. Sitting at her desk, Berta lowered her head to the wood grain and let out a low sigh. Of course, she knew right away that it could only be one person. If Papa had meant to let her stay, then surely he would have simply returned her letter with his signature of permission. Showing up at the convent himself could only mean a few things, and none of them were good.

Berta collected herself and trailed the sister downstairs. Sure enough, her Papa was waiting there, with Gretel in tow. The man caught Berta in his gaze as soon as she had descended the stairs. Gretel, however, refused to make eye contact of any sort, instead focusing on the sparse decoration of the sitting room, feigning fascination in the simple architecture. At this Berta could not help but be amused. Perhaps, Berta considered, she had taught Gretel a lesson after all.

Papa, was strung tight as a violin. He seemed to vibrate subtly as he moved—such was the rigidity of his motion. They all sat together in the common room. The silence went on for a time before any one of them worked up the nerve to break it.

"If there are any belongings Berta must collect, it would be best if she did that now," Papa finally broke in. "She will be returning home with us immediately." This, Papa addressed to no one in particular, neither Berta nor the nun who sat with them. Instead the words hung in the middle of the room, drifting slowly down to the floor.

"But Papa—" Berta began to plead, cleverly addressing him as if she were still a child.

"Nein Berta," Papa interjected; the tone in his voice quelled any further protestation Berta might lobby.

After feeling like she had finally found her place,

Berta was faced once more with the realization that she belonged nowhere. She was to go back to her Papa's house, knowing very well that it was no longer her home. If she was truthful with herself, it hadn't really felt like home since her mother passed. Surely now, after her bout with Gretel, life would be made as difficult for her as possible.

Collecting her things and saying a brief and tearful goodbye to the woman she had spent the past 3 years in the seminary alongside, Berta loaded into her Papa's truck and began the journey back home.

The trip was silent. Berta sat wedged against the door of the truck with Gretel sitting silently beside her. Gretel still had not provided any indication that she even noticed Berta was there.

As they arrived home, Papa opened the door for Gretel—not seeming to care whether or not Berta followed. Berta moved to her old bedroom and placed her suitcase on the bed. Turning back towards the door, she noticed her

Papa standing there.

"Tomorrow you will find a job, and you will find a new place to live. I will not have you in my house for any longer than is strictly necessary. Are we understood?"

Berta never unpacked her suitcase. Standing with her coat fastened tightly around her, she stood in the bedroom and listened quietly for the footsteps and latch of the door that would signify her Papa and Gretel had gone to bed. Once she heard the telltale shuffling of feet—the clicking of the bolt—she quietly departed her room and moved to the front door. Turning the knob slowly, then jerking the door open to avoid the creaking hinges, Berta slipped out into the night.

The thumping of her suitcase against her knee reminded Berta of the night four years prior when she had walked nearly the same path by her brother's side. She wondered wistfully where he might be now and what he was doing. Elongating her strides, Berta picked up her pace as she made her way along the three kilometers to the local child welfare office.

From the outside, the building looked quite shabby. The paint was peeling; the metal sign dented as though somebody had scored a direct hit with a hefty rock. Worst of all, the light that overhung the front entrance was either broken or burned out. Berta slumped against the side of the building with only the light of the moon to keep her company. Wishing she still had Ed's jacket for added warmth, she tried to close her eyes and will the morning to arrive.

A nudging of her foot woke Berta from her restless sleep. A woman hovered over her, gently poking at Berta with the tip of her shoe. Struggling to adjust to the early morning light, Berta's hazy eyes could hardly make out the shape of the woman standing before her. Collecting her belongings off the ground and dusting herself off, Berta followed the woman into the office. The light comfortably dim once inside, Berta's eyes adjusted enough to notice the woman's features. It was the very same social worker who had shown up on their stoop after the passing of Berta's mother. She hoped that the woman did not remember the harsh treatment to which she had been subjected to by Berta's Papa.

The woman recognized Berta immediately, giving no indication as to her recollection of past cruelties. Berta explained her situation to the woman. The story itself was not much different than what she had told the elderly woman the day after she first left home, or the one she had told to the nun that afternoon on the park bench. Now the story was a bit longer, but Berta had grown used to the intricacies of its telling.

"If you enjoyed your time at the convent, I know of another at which you can stay until you're twenty-one. It is a ways away and would require us to take a train. If you're interested, I could make a quick phone call and bring you there this morning."

"Will it matter that I'm only seventeen? I won't be able to get my Papa's permission." Berta interjected.

"This is a different kind of convent. A place that specializes in situations such as yours. Your Papa's permission will not be necessary."

Berta couldn't believe what she was hearing, it sounded too good to be true. With few other options, she thought it best to take the woman at her word. She expressed her desire to leave as soon as possible. The woman led her to a waiting room and disappeared back into her office.

Next Phase

The train ride lasted for hours. Berta sat with her coat wedged between her head and the glass window. Sitting across from Berta, the social worker stared absentmindedly out the window as the countryside floated passed. Too afraid to ask where exactly it was that they were going, Berta tried to relax and prepare herself for the next phase of her journey.

As the train came to a stop, Berta realized that she was as far away from her hometown as she had ever been. Everything felt different, even the air smelled a bit off. It turned out the convent was within walking distance of the train station. Though many years the woman's junior, Berta's strides were much greater than those of the stout social worker. Shortening her pace, Berta attempted to let the woman lead.

Arriving at what had been described to her as a "convent," Berta immediately felt a sinking feeling in her chest. The place looked much—to her eyes—like a prison. From the outside she noticed the tall, sturdy walls and the windows encased in thick iron bars. Walking through the front door confirmed any shred of doubt that Berta may have harbored about the place. The walls were white. The decoration meager, at best. It reminded Berta of the time spent visiting her mother in the hospital. The tile floors gleamed in contrast to the drab uniforms worn by the few children she could spot from the front entrance. Berta turned quickly on her heel—figuring that it might be her last chance to leave the place, whatever it might be. Just then she felt a hand on her shoulder; a woman in a white uniform clamped her hand onto Berta and directed her into the next room, closing the door behind them.

Berta sat in the strange little waiting room. She could hear the muted voices of the social worker speaking with the woman in the white uniform from behind the door. Finally, the uniformed woman reentered the room and ordered Berta to collect her things and follow closely behind her.

The initial impressions Berta had of the place were proving to be more and more accurate, the farther she moved into the building. They arrived in a long room housing ten beds. The narrow windows, cut into the walls at regular intervals, were covered with bars just the same as the ones that Berta had seen from outside.

"This is where you will be staying," the woman brayed. "I suggest the bed at the far end of the room. Put your things underneath. You will not be permitted to enter or leave any room in this building without being accompanied by one of the staff. Get settled quickly, the other children will be returning soon." Without any further explanation, she removed herself from the room, leaving Berta alone. As the door closed, Berta noticed that there was no handle on the inside. She couldn't let herself out if she wanted to, and she wanted to very much.

Days at the Orphanage

Days at the orphanage were monotonous. Berta fell into the schedule of her day and tried her best to ignore the uncomfortable confines of her surroundings. She was up at six every morning. A staff member would gather up all ten children for breakfast. The meal was never exciting, but Berta ate. Not long after her arrival, it was explained to her that she would be kept at the orphanage until she was twenty-one—possibly earlier if she behaved herself and demonstrated good work ethic. Making the best of her time was the only rational thing to do.

After breakfast, Berta was led to another wing of the building where she spent the remainder of her day watching after the younger children, as well as those that were mentally and physically handicapped. At this, Berta excelled. Having cared for her younger brother growing up, she had acquired a patient, nurturing nature. The children loved her, and spending time with them helped her days ease by. The initial anger she felt at her predicament subsided with time, and she grew to accept her new home and the rewards of watching the young ones grow.

Having earned the trust of the staff, Berta soon found herself with new accommodations. A small, semi-private room to be shared with just one other girl. A bed, a writing desk and a small dresser fit themselves neatly on Berta's side of the room. With her new space came added freedoms: allowed to move freely between the showers, kitchen and laundry, Berta felt herself shedding the underlying feeling of claustrophobia she had harbored subconsciously since her arrival.

At the orphanage, the highlight of every year was surely the annual Christmas party thrown by the wives of the American military base nearby. The main hall in which the children ate their meals was transformed into a holiday spectacle: tables and chairs were moved to the sides of the room; banners and paper streamers filled the space with a festive atmosphere, and in the center of it all was the meticulously curated tree, decorated to the fullest by a swarm of bustling volunteers. Berta liked to watch the women as they worked, ears attuned to the strangeness of their accents and the clicking of their shoes on the tiled floor.

Berta enjoyed nothing more than to see the faces of the children as the doors to the dining hall were opened on Christmas morning. Little eyes reflected the twinkling of the lights; while their smiles seemed to make the entire room glow. Sitting to the side of the room, Berta assisted the smallest children with the unwrapping of their gifts. Soon, she was covered in shredded paper and string, basking in the sounds of the children fawning over new toys. A hand on her shoulder jolted her out of her reverie.

"Berta, could you follow me please?" The stern voice came from the woman in charge of the orphanage, Ms. Waechter. Berta rarely had any occasion to interact with her and was surprised by the sudden request.

"Yes ma'am," Berta offered submissively as she followed Ms. Waechter to her office just down the hall from the festivities in the dining room.

Entering the dimly lit office, Berta noticed an impeccably dressed American woman seated across from the desk. Her back towards Berta and Ms. Waechter, the woman shifted uncomfortably in her seat.

"Ahem," Ms. Waechter cleared her throat. "Mrs. Reiling, this is the girl about whom we spoke earlier." Surprised by the break in the silence, the woman flinched briefly before springing energetically to her feet and turning to face Berta. "Why hello there Ms…," she muttered demurely. "Who might you be?"

"Berta, ma'am," she replied.

"Please, call me Mrs. Reiling."

Ms. Waechter directed Berta to sit. Berta smiled shyly towards Mrs. Reiling as Ms. Waechter assumed her own position behind the desk.

"Berta," Ms. Waechter spoke, a businesslike tone in her voice. "Mrs. Reiling came to me this morning in hopes that I might have a girl that would be willing to come and work for her as a live in maid, to assist in taking care of her three small children. After the splendid job that you have done here in looking after the children, I thought you might be just the right fit for the job." Flattered, Berta looked from Ms. Waechter to Mrs. Reiling and back again. Lost for words, her mind raced with the prospects of the opportunity that had been presented to her. She would be able to leave the orphanage early, with a place to live and a little money in her pocket. Her eyes swam at the thought of it. Sensing she was allowing the moment to drag on awkwardly, she cleared her throat, looking back and forth between the two women, unsure of whom to address.

"I would love the opportunity," She split the difference between the two women, speaking toward the middle of the room—hoping not to offend either.

"Splendid," chirped Mrs. Reiling, clasping her hands together as if to put a physical seal on the transaction.

Gasping for Breath

Goodbyes at the orphanage were brief. Though she had spent just over two years of her life within its walls, Berta had not formed any sort of deep attachment to the place. She felt a fleeting pang of grief at leaving the children behind, but understood that they would move on quickly. At their age, every day was awash with more discoveries and information than their young brains could reasonably keep up with. She reconciled with becoming a part of the technicolor fuzz of that memory.

The Reiling's apartment was located in a large barracks residential building, full of military families. The building itself was a sickly sort of pale green. Its first three floors served as military dwellings, with quarters for the live in help, situated just under the sloping the roof.

Mrs. Reiling led Berta to the top floor. Being the middle of the day, it was fairly empty—as the other girls, with whom Berta would be living, were going about their duties. Berta was led into a decent sized room, respectably furnished, of which the far wall sloped drastically to account for the roof. A small, four-paned window overlooked the car lot and adjacent trees. Berta was struck with disbelief as Mrs. Reiling assured her that the room was, indeed, just for her. Placing her suitcase gingerly on the bed, so as not to muss the tightly pulled bedspread, Berta removed her jacket and followed Mrs. Reiling back out. Just before the door swung fully closed, Berta took one last look to assure herself that her eyes had not been playing tricks.

Entering the residence proper, Mrs. Reiling and Berta were greeted by three young children—all nicely put together and in a row. A harried looking nurse, who had been keeping an eye on the children while Mrs. Reiling was out fetching Berta, scooted past them and out the door with a quick nod of recognition to each. The children were introduced as Timothy, Patricia, and Robert—ages ten, eight and seven, respectively. As well behaved and fastidiously groomed as they seemed, Berta had an inkling that they might prove to be a handful.

The rest of the day was spent better acquainting herself with the children, and taking mental notes as

Mrs. Reiling showed her the ins and outs of the apartment. Running the house while taking care of three mischievous children during the day was sure to be a new challenge.

At the end of the work day, Berta wandered back up to her room and flung herself down on her new bed. Pleased with how quickly her life had changed and fading quickly towards sleep, Berta was awoken by voices from down the hall. Poking her head from the doorway, she noticed that the other live in girls had arrived back from their day's work as well. Slipping down the hall to the large center room, Berta nervously introduced herself to the group. Everyone was receptive to Berta, and she began talking and laughing with her new roommates immediately.

Berta was informed that they were required to work from six in the morning until six in the evening, but everything after that was free time. Unused to a schedule and living arrangements that allowed for such freedom, Berta lavished in the girls talk of going to movies and plays in their free time. She could hardly wait to take advantage of everything her new life had to offer.

Spontaneity had never before been a part of Berta's lexicon. The idea that any given Saturday evening could offer up the possibility of music, dancing and inebriated laughter was, to Berta, some kind of alchemy. Adrenaline from the delightful impossibility she found herself in was enough to keep her warm through the walk to the local pub.

Berta tried to keep up as her three compatriots bustled up ahead. Sabine, Brigitte and Eva were certainly the most outgoing of the girls that Berta boarded with. Being the new girl in the house, Berta was determined to do her very best to keep up with them. They linked arms as they gossiped and giggled their way down the street—looking like one great bundled mass; plumes of dewy breath wreathing their heads.

Sabine twisted her dark hair around a finger, letting it twirl and fall repeatedly as she sipped her drink. Berta could hardly stand the smell of alcohol, let alone the taste. She sipped on a cola as her friends drank. At the adjacent table sat four ruggedly handsome local men. Brigitte noticed them before the others, nudging Eva and Berta in hopes of alerting them to the presence of the men.

"The one with the curly hair is staring right at you Berta!" Brigitte crooned.

"Not so loud," chided Berta, her face red from embarrassment and the warmth of the pub. She glanced quickly in the direction of the German men, hoping to catch a quick peek without them noticing.

"I bet every last one of you a drink that he asks me to dance first," blurted Sabine. Eva, being more shy than Berta, giggled nervously in subtle agreement.

"I don't know, Sabine, I think he has eyes for this one." Brigitte wiggled herself closer to Berta, gently nudging her once again.

"All of you stop before they hear us." Berta shot them all a quick look before focusing her gaze on the lazy bubbles of the soda on the table in front of her.

As it turned out, Berta would win that bet after all. Still gazing demurely down at her drink, she felt the other girls straighten themselves up and go quiet. Feeling a tap on her shoulder, Berta turned around slowly—knowing that she would face the inevitable prospect of the curly headed man standing right behind her. Sure enough, there he was, offering her his hand. The actual desire to dance with him paled in comparison to the chance of showing up Sabine; Berta wearily grasped his hand and followed him to the dance floor.

Disliking it as she did, Berta's nose was keenly attuned to the smell of alcohol. As they danced and the man pulled her closer, she could almost see the alcohol emanating from his mouth in waves. Two things became immediately evident: the man was severely intoxicated, and he had more on his mind than dancing alone. Being pulled closer still, Berta became aware of the tiniest details of the man's appearance: Sweat that beaded over his upper lip; a spot of dried blood under his chin where he had nicked himself with his razor while shaving.

"Come home with me." His voice authoritative, less a question than a statement. Though his eyes were shrouded behind an alcoholic glaze, Berta could still see something in there that didn't sit quite right with her.

"My friends are leaving soon. I really need to be getting back," Berta offered, hopefully—thinking she may not be fortunate enough to get off that easy. His hand tightened to the back of her dress.

"I wasn't asking," he sneered. His lip quivered slightly to reveal a menacing half smile. Then he gripped her arm, twisting it behind her back and leading her in the direction of the front door. Being half his size, Berta was helpless to resist. Her struggle futile as the door grew closer.

Too scared even to let the scream that was rising in her chest make its way to her mouth, Berta felt the bracing winter air against her face as she was pushed out the door. The front of the pub being well lit, with other patrons coming and going, the man dragged her across the street. The light from the street lamps failed to illuminate past the initial copse of trees, leaving the majority of the park draped in darkness.

Throwing Berta to the ground, the man dropped to his knees, pinned her with one arm, and unclasped his belt. Berta was lost; her mind swimming, left clutching at clumps of stiff, frozen grass. Though she swung at his face, it proved to be just out of reach due to the length of his arms. She shuddered as each inhalation provided another lungful of his repulsive breath.

"You asked for this—the way you were dancing with me," he growled. "You must have known you had this coming."

When he was finished, he lifted himself back to his knees and fastened his belt with one hand as he re-tucked his shirt with the other. Berta drew her knees to her chest. She pressed her face to the cold earth, gasping for breath through the pain.

The man stumbled as he rose to his feet, bracing

himself against a nearby tree for support.

"You're probably pregnant now," he spat. He fixed his hair as he wandered, unsteadily, back towards the bar, looking as if what he had just done was already gone from his mind. Berta watched him go without lifting her head from the ground.

It took her a few minutes to pull herself up from the grass. Fixing her dress as best she could, she wiped her face. The only words that rung through her buzzing brain were her Papa's: warning her against ever kissing a boy, lest she become pregnant. Terrified, cold and shaking, she wandered back out of the park.

Out of all the girls in the house, Berta felt closest to Brigitte. Calling her into the bedroom the next morning before work, Berta divulged everything that had happened the night before. At first, Brigitte didn't say anything, she just sat and held Berta tight.

"Berta, whatever you do, you can't tell Mrs. Reiling."

Brigitte held Berta at arm's length—looking her in the eye to ensure she understood what she was hearing. "The Reilings are Catholic. As nice as she seems, she'll run you out if she finds out that you're going to be a single mother. The best thing you can do is wait it out and hope that it doesn't take." Brigitte averted her eyes after this, hating to be the first to tell Berta the facts.

Within a few weeks, Berta was constantly sick. Mrs. Reiling came to fetch her one morning when she was late for work. After knocking several times, she found Berta hovering over the toilet, obviously unwell. Berta was only able to keep the charade going for a couple of weeks after that. She knew that soon she'd start showing, and she wanted nothing more than to avoid the embarrassment of seeing the look on Mrs. Reiling's face as she found out the news.

With a little help from Sabine, Berta was able to locate a small room for rent in town. However, the little money that she had been able to save would only carry her for a limited amount of time. So, Berta adopted a daily routine of scouring the town for work. She would rise early and return to her room as the sky turned dark. Now that her pregnancy had started to show, she knew it would be more difficult to find a steady job. Proprietors' judgmental glances upon noticing her state were discouraging, but still Berta carried on, knowing she would soon be providing support for two.

Eating for Two

It was becoming increasingly evident that Berta was now eating for two. Hoping to stave off pangs of hunger for a while longer, Berta finally gave in to the cavernous rumbling of her stomach and stopped for lunch at a hot dog stand. While waiting in line, Berta clutched at her midsection, wrapping her coat tighter in hopes of stifling her stomach's growing protestations. Turning her attention to the cart, her mouth began to water with the promise of nourishment. She suddenly noticed the young attendant at the stand.

The girl was not much older than Berta, sporting curly brown locks and a conspicuous bulge beneath her apron. Berta thought it a strange coincidence that she would happen upon another young mother to be. She took some relief in encountering another bound by her same set of circumstances. As the man in front of her cleared out, munching happily, Berta approached the cart.

"Just one please." Berta smiled.

"One mark," the girl replied wearily. Not knowing

whether to pursue the conversation based on the girl's rather wan response, Berta began to fish the change from her pocket.

"When are you due?" Berta offered in hopes that it might spark the girls interest, and enlighten her to the fact that Berta was in a similar predicament. Sure enough, the girl snapped from the haze of her drudgery—eyes wandering over Berta before finally alighting on her recently rounded stomach.

"A little more than four months now," muttering weakly, but managing to work up an unconvincing smile. The girl prepared Berta's hot dog as she spoke. "And you?"

"Around six months or so, I would imagine." Berta replied. "Your husband must be hoping for a boy?" Berta inquired in attempt to elongate the conversation. There were no others in line, and Berta was grateful to have found somebody with whom she shared a common experience. She thought there would be no harm in trying to befriend the girl or at least borrow a sympathetic ear for a few moments.

"Oh...I'm...I'm not married." The girl shrugged, embarrassed. Handing Berta her food, she wiped her hands across her apron and began to fiddle nervously with the cart.

"Don't worry, neither am I." Berta said, watching as the girl's body language eased considerably. "To tell you the God's honest truth, I was attacked by a man. It was him that did this to me." At this, the girl's head snapped to attention. Berta, caught off guard by the sudden attentiveness of her companion, wondered if she had struck a nerve.

"Were you attacked here in town?" the girl questioned. "I was...in the park outside a pub. It was dark, no one was around."

"Did he have dark curly hair?" the girl was pale. She paused between words as her mouth went dry.

"Yes...," Berta replied, gravely.

"The best thing that you could do for both yourself and your baby is to get out of town if you're able," spoke the girl. At this, the blood drained from Berta's face.

"He has been searching for me. A friend of mine, who I was with that night, ran into him. He is a married man and he wants to knock the baby from my belly so his wife will never find out. If you can, leave soon. I would if I had the means or anyplace else to go."

Berta nodded to assure the girl she had received the message loud and clear. Bidding the girl watch out for her own safety, and that of her child. Berta hurried back to her room, dropping her hot dog along the way. She had enough money left for a train ticket. Though it was the last thing in the world she wanted to do, if it meant the safety of her child, she had no other choice.

Having already knocked on her Papa's door twice with no answer, she had begun to wonder if anyone was home. Berta knocked for the third time.

"COME IN!" Berta cringed as she heard her Papa's voice. Opening the door slowly, so as not to raise her Papa's ire any more than need be, Berta entered and caught her Papa's eye immediately. She watched as his gaze dipped down to her belly and rose back up, full of fire, to meet her own.

Before Berta even had a chance to open her mouth, her Papa's belt was loosed from around his trousers. Crouching to the floor, raising one hand to her face and dropping the other to her stomach, Berta turned her body away from her father just as the first of the blows fell.

"I warned you to...never"—a blow across Berta's back—"...get..." a glancing strike that nipped at the edge of her ear "...pregnant!" Papa punctuated his statement with a flurry of snapping blows, the leather whistling through the air. Berta experienced a sensation of deja vu as, breathing heavily, her Papa worked his belt back through the loop of his trousers and fastened it in place.

"You can stay here until the child is born. Then you will find a job and get out of my house." Papa barked.

Pulling herself from the floor and picking up her fallen luggage, Berta turned to move back towards her old bedroom. As she moved past her Papa he grabbed her roughly by the upper arm, halting her progress. "Are we clear," he growled.

"Y—Yes." Berta choked back a whimper before responding in as strong a manner as she could muster. Tugging her arm lose from his grasp, she proceeded back to the bedroom. Berta shut the door behind her before seating herself on the bed and weeping silently.

Father did not speak another word to Berta until her child was born several months later. A midwife had been called to the house to assist with the birth. During labor, the baby had gotten turned around—a situation that was beyond the expertise of the midwife and necessitated the arrival of a doctor. Eventually, the baby was delivered, a little girl named Konnie.

The midwife patted Berta's forehead with a damp cloth as the doctor checked the baby to make sure that she was breathing correctly. Seeing her child for the first time, Berta couldn't help but smile. No matter the circumstances by which she arrived, she was beautiful and Berta longed to hold the child in her arms. The doctor severed the cord before handing her off to the midwife. Berta looked on as the midwife gently cleaned and swaddled the now crying infant. No sooner had the child been wrapped in its blanket, then Papa swept in to intercept the child—clutching her to his chest.

"Under no circumstances will you be allowed to care for, or even hold, this child." Papa stated to a still delirious Berta. "You can't be trusted to care for yourself. I don't know where you possibly got the idea that you were prepared to care for a child. As soon as you are out of bed, you will find a job and get out of my house. We will take care of the child." With those final words, Papa stormed from the room with the baby, leaving Berta in a horrified daze.

The midwife, having completed her duties, let herself out. Berta was left alone once again, without even the company of the child who she had carried with her for so many months. Exhausted, she could no longer summon the energy to fight back her tears. Drawing the bed covers to her face, she wept inconsolably. When she finally caught her breath, she lowered the covers and noticed a blurry figure in the doorway. Dabbing at her eyes with the sheet, Berta cleared her vision enough to recognize that is was Gretel. Staring stone faced from the doorway, Gretel did not move even once as she noticed Berta staring back. Finally, her stony visage cracked and broke into the gruesome smile Berta knew so well. The only thought that floated through Berta's hazy mind was that this was the face of the devil.

Out for Thirty Days

After recovering from her pregnancy, Berta was quickly able to find work and a small room for rent in town. Working at a nearby cork factory, she was able to make twenty-five marks per week—the bulk of the paycheck going to her father to help him take care of her daughter, Konnie. When all was said and done, Berta was left with roughly five marks.

Work at the factory was wearisome. Dust from the cutting tables spouted into the air, swirling in the light from the tall windows that lined the factory floor. Berta worked in a line with many other women in front of a large table saw. As the cork slid along the conveyor belt, it was up to Berta to put a notch in each piece using the loud buzzing saw in front of her. After she returned home in the evenings, it took Berta many hours to dispel that buzzing sound from her ears.

Berta felt her cheeks flush and shifted her weight across the uncomfortable stool on which she spent her days. With what little was left of her weekly paychecks, she had not been feeding herself well. On most days her diet consisted of banana sandwiches and vanilla pudding. Berta attributed the pain in her abdomen to hunger, having grown used to the gurgling, twisting sensation of a stomach that was begging for nourishment. She turned all her attention on her work, attempting to will the discomfort away.

Focusing on the seemingly endless line of cork meandering down the table, Berta felt her vision momentarily cross and blur—one line became several until she shook her head, attempting to clear the cobwebs. As she diverted her attention back to her hands, she felt a drop of sweat slowly winding its way down her nose before dropping in front of her. She could feel the back of her throat growing slick as the feeling of inevitable sickness swept over her, warming her entire body.

"Berta," the co-worker nearest to her shouted over the drone of the machinery, "are you alright?" The question posed in response to the color draining completely from Berta's once rosy face. "Yes... fine." Berta nodded, smiling weakly. She fumbled absently with the piece of cork she clutched in her hands.

"I'm going to call the supervisor, you don't look well," the woman assured her.

"No," cautioned Berta, swallowing hard. "I can't afford to miss the day of work." "Nonsense, you look like death." The woman rose to find the man who ran the factory. Just then Berta dipped her head unconsciously, catching herself momentarily before blacking out altogether—her head slapping the table just in front of the large saw.

"Berta!" the co-workers startled scream managed to pierce the cacophony of the floor, alerting several other women who had been lost in their work. Leaping to Berta's side, the woman dragged her from the table moments before the saw would have bitten into the exposed flesh of her cheek. Proving too weak to handle Berta's unconscious form, the woman lost her hold and Berta slipped to the floor—motionless and breathing shallowly.

Raising an alarm that shut down every saw on the line, the supervisor rushed to call an ambulance. An eerie calm fell over the room which had, only moments before, been filled with the sounds of labor. Berta lay limp on the floor, not to be woken even by the whining of the approaching ambulance.

After spending a brief time in the hospital, it was determined that Berta was suffering from a fever. She was sent home to rest. Papa worked, which left Konnie home alone with Gretel.

While sequestered in her bedroom, Berta wandered in and out of consciousness. The snippets of Konnie's cries that she could hear from her bed lifted her spirits momentarily, only to bring them crashing back down with the realization that her daughter had been left alone with Gretel. Try as she might, Berta could not summon the strength to raise herself from the bed. The light, or absence thereof, emanating from the shaded window was the only proof Berta had that time was passing at all.

Ed arrived three days in to Berta's bed rest. Letting himself in to her darkened bedchamber, he was struck by the pungent odor of sickness. Hastily approaching Berta's shrouded form, he lifted the covers to find that they were soaked through with sweat. Damp and heavy, he peeled the bedding back from Berta's pale and shivering body.

"Berta," Ed implored "Berta are you awake?" To this her eyelids fluttered briefly. She recognized Ed's face, thinking that it was now the second time that she had been saved by her brother. He could hear the sound accompanying her effort to dislodge her tongue from the dried roof of her mouth. Berta fought to speak, but, to Ed, her attempts were completely incomprehensible. Panicking, Ed rushed to the kitchen where his Papa sat with Gretel.

"Has nobody been looking in on her? She looks near death!" Ed yelped, disbelief impinging on his speech. Disgusted at the seeming lack of concern, Ed rushed to call an ambulance for Berta.

Berta roused briefly, ears attuned to the commotion that Ed was raising down the hall. Her thoughts flitted briefly to Konnie, before they were consumed by the fever in her brow. She felt a draft from the door blowing cool air over her sweat slicked skin. She knew she should be cold, but she burned too intensely for it to cause her much bother. Then, unable to muster the energy, she slipped back into sleep.

She awoke to bright lights refracted from the white walls of a barren room. A man's face hovered in her vision. His glasses reflecting the light, making it impossible to see his eyes. The scent of disinfectant triggered memories of the last visits she shared with her mother.

"She lives," jested the man, perhaps a bit insensitively. Berta's eyes had adjusted well enough that she could see that he wore a white coat; presumably, he was her doctor. "You gave everyone quite a scare young lady."

"Hm," Berta heard her woozy voice, coughed twice to

clear her throat before venturing on "how long?" Still muttering, but coherent enough that the doctor could follow her train of thought.

"You've been out for thirty days as of today. You were quite ill." Scribbling something on a clipboard, the doctor looked up to shoot her a quick smile.

"The fever? I was asleep for a month because of a fever?" Berta questioned. "Oh no, my dear. It seems that whoever presided over the delivery of your child failed to remove the afterbirth. This can be very dangerous and was so; in your case. Putting you in a coma for the better part of a month."

Berta couldn't believe that she had been unconscious for an entire month. Raising her hand to her brow, she noticed that it shook with weakness.

"We've put you on antibiotics to clear up the remainder of the infection, but it would be best if you stayed here for a while yet so we can observe your progress a bit longer." The doctor explained, absentmindedly tapping his pen against the golden frame of his glasses.

"How much longer will I need to stay?" asked Berta, nervous to hear his answer. "A week or so should be sufficient, as long as everything goes to plan," he replied. "But, my daughter...I need to get back to work. I've already been gone a month, I must get back as soon as possible." Berta pleaded.

"The risk of the infection returning is still too high. If we release you now, and the infection returns, it may make it difficult for you to conceive in the future," cautioned the doctor, taking a paternal tone.

"I will have to take that risk," Berta replied. "I have to get back home as soon as possible."

"Understand that leaving now is most certainly against my recommendation." he stated, "But if you must, I can hardly stop you."

"Thank you, doctor." Berta thought of her daughter and of the time she had already missed with her. She thought of the factory job, which was surely lost to her after a month long absence. She vowed to get her strength back as quickly as she possibly could.

Elisabeth B. Couture

Something was Different

As she feared, Berta's position at the cork factory did not hold itself for her as she recovered from her illness. If it were ever in doubt, Berta's father made it abundantly clear he did not want her in the house from the moment she returned from the hospital. Still weak from her long stretch of inactivity, Berta had a long road to regaining her full strength. Venturing further and further from the house each day, her search for work lasted only as long as her legs would allow. By her second week out of the hospital, her strength had returned enough to allow her access to the neighboring town where she found a kind elderly couple who took to her right away. They offered her a position in their bar. Sympathizing with her predicament, they allowed her a small advance in order to secure a room just down the street.

Berta enjoyed the lively atmosphere of the bar. Even if she still couldn't stand the smell of alcohol, she learned to live with it. She found herself growing quite popular with certain patrons, and was often thankful to have the protective barrier of the bar between herself and the rowdy customers. There was, however, one American soldier who had proven himself to be a regular and a different case altogether.

The first time he showed up, with his close cropped hair and American swagger, Berta treated him as any other customer.

"What can I get for you?" Berta inquired, businesslike but friendly, as she was with any customer who had not given her a reason to be otherwise.

"I'll have a beer please," the soldier replied. Berta thought that she'd never quite get used to the sound of an American's accent. She got his beer, skimming the extra foam off the top as she slid the mug to the man over the bar.

"Thank you," the man smiled, confident, but polite. Berta thought him unlike the cocky, arrogant, and oftentimes rude American soldiers she encountered on a daily basis; something was different about this one. She flashed him a smile, taking note of the warmth in the face that gazed back at her.

Berta had the following day off. She rose early in the morning, nearly rising with the sun. Gretel had promised to bring Konnie by for a visit, and though Berta didn't want to get her hopes up too high, she ultimately failed in her attempts to stifle her excitement. Though she was tidy by nature, Berta found herself checking things over two and three times, just to make sure they were perfect: making her bed just to tear it apart completely and replacing the sheets so they fell smooth—the creases at the corners just right. When she was sure that nothing was out of place, all dust and dirt thoroughly eradicated, she donned her coat and left for the shop.

Opportunities to see her daughter being rare, Berta wanted to be sure she made as good an impression as possible on her baby girl. Browsing through the shop just down the street from her room, she picked out a stuffed bear. The velveteen; pads of its feet matching the light pink polka dots of the ribbon it wore around its neck, Berta thought it perfect. Worrying that Gretel might arrive early to find her gone, Berta fumbled with her change in her haste to pay the clerk. Rushing back home, Berta was relieved to find that Gretel and Konnie had not yet arrived.

Placing the bear just so on the dresser by her bed, Berta sat down carefully on her perfectly made bedspread, swiped a hand across her dress to remove any unwanted wrinkles, and trained her eyes on the door.

A single knock at the door was all it took for Berta to fly across the room, swinging the door open with enough force to upset Gretel's brittle hair as she stood in the hallway, and earning an approving giggle from Konnie. With an obligatory nod to Gretel, Berta ushered them both inside. Gretel seated herself in the single chair the room had to offer and handed Konnie off to an eager Berta. Berta, sitting Konnie on the rug that covered the length of the room, rose to retrieve the gift she had purchased for her daughter. Delighted by the softness of the toy bear, Konnie cooed in appreciation as tears welled in Berta's eyes.

"Thank you," Berta offered to Gretel, opening the

door. Occupied with Konnie, Berta had managed to avoid speaking to Gretel until the moment they had to depart. "Here is some money for Konnie," Berta contributed what she could—a healthy amount of the pay she earned at the bar.

"I will bring Konnie to visit every month if you keep up with payments," said Gretel, breaking her silence. "If you fail to provide money for your daughter, I will stop bringing her here."

"Don't worry, I have a steady job. It won't be a problem." Berta could hear the pleading tone in her voice and hated herself for it. She wondered when she might finally free herself from under the boot of this woman.

Kissing Konnie goodbye, Berta watched as Gretel carried her back down the hall. She hoped that Gretel would stay true to her word, as Berta planned to stay true to her own.

Two months went by, Gretel upheld her promise,

bringing Konnie to visit with Berta twice more. Likewise, Berta made sure she had money to send back home with Gretel each time.

At the bar, Berta had grown used to the appearance of the polite American soldier. He had taken to coming into the bar twice a week. On each visit after the first, he had arrived with a box of chocolates, roses and the request for Berta to join him for a movie. Flattered as she was, she rebuffed his advances each time. Although, as time went on, Berta allowed herself to admit that the man's persistence impressed her.

Striding to the counter—a box of chocolates clutched under one arm and holding a half dozen roses in his hand—the American took the same seat he sat in every week. Berta noticed him immediately, though she pretended not to. She turned quickly back towards the cash register, pitching her head down in an attempt to conceal her smile. Composing herself, she approached the man who seemingly refused to rest until he won her over.

"I do not even know your name," Berta stated, glibly. "You show up at this bar twice a week and today it's with roses and candy that I never asked for, and you still haven't told me your name."

"Joseph," he said, extending his hand out over the counter "and yours?"

"Berta," grasping his hand in return, she failed to hide her smile any longer. This man had succeeded, though she had tried to avoid it, in breaking through the wall she had raised around herself.

"So, Berta, now that we're acquainted, will you see a movie with me?" Smiling confidently, Joseph knew his persistence had paid off. He could not remember anybody smiling at him quite like that, not ever.

"Oh, fine. I suppose," grumbled Berta, feigning exasperation.

"Friday evening?" Joseph asked.

"If we must," Berta grinned. Try as she might, she could not wipe the smile from her face. She had lost the upper hand, and she was not upset about it.

In fact, she felt just the opposite.

Returning from the bar later that evening, Berta was surprised to find her Papa standing patiently outside her door.

"Berta, I have something to discuss with you," her Papa intoned, his voice was grave and serious. As Berta opened the door to let him in, she was struck with fear.

"Is something the matter with Konnie?" Berta gulped, wide eyed.

"No, Berta; Konnie is fine." I came here to tell you that it's time to start helping out with some money for Konnie. Gretel and I are doing it on our own. I shouldn't have to come here and ask for your help. She is your daughter, after all." He clenched his fists as he spoke; Berta could feel his anger—she'd seen it enough in the past. Yet, she was in disbelief.

"Did you know that Gretel brings Konnie to visit me once a month?" Berta bravely held her ground.

"I did, and for that kindness we still receive no help from you," Papa replied.

"Then she must've failed to tell you that each time she visits, I've given her one hundred marks to help with Konnie's care. I have been setting aside money from my job at the bar. If you'd like you can ask the owners; they've been helping me to save and have seen me pay Gretel personally."

Knowing that she had the upper hand, Berta couldn't help but enjoy the feeling of watching her Papa deflate. Finally, Berta was able to make her Papa see Gretel as she had seen her since the first time they met.

"Gretel has been lying to you. If you'd like me to

prove it to you, I would be happy to."

"No...hm," her Papa stammered "that won't be necessary."

Without so much as a goodbye, her Papa turned in defeat, closing the door behind him as he left.

Berta, true to her word, accompanied Joseph to see a movie the following Friday. As they sat in the theater, Berta was thankful that she didn't have to attempt an awkward conversation. Instead they just sat, in the dark, enjoying each other's company. Once the movie let out, Joseph held the door for Berta as they left the theater.

Taking Joseph up on his offer to accompany her back home, Berta walked by his side feeling like a bundle of nerves. Words rushed through her head too quickly to pin down. Each time she thought of something to say, it seemed too ridiculous, or trivial, so she remained silent. Little did she know, the very same thoughts ran through Joseph's head.

They struck quite the pair, strolling silently down the road. Finally arriving at Berta's apartment, after what felt to her like an eternity, she turned to Joseph—still unsure. "What is the one thing that you would like to do, if you could do anything?" Joseph asked her.

"Umm..." caught off guard by the sudden question, Berta struggled to respond. In her haste, she fell back on honesty.

"I would like to go spend some time with my daughter."

Though she had mentioned Konnie to him before, she still had no idea how he might handle the response. "Then next week I'd like to take you to see you're little girl, if you'd like?" He responded without missing a beat, surprising Berta and rendering her all but speechless.

"Yes...yes I would love that," she stammered.

"Then it's a date. Goodnight then," he declared.

Berta's Beginnings

Taking her head in his hands, he planted a kiss in the middle of her forehead and turned, to head back down the street.

The lights of the restaurant were dim, flickering briefly as the wind whipped by the window outside. Rain spattered against glass window, rapping against the roof as if to punctuate the low hum of chatter that carried throughout the room. Joseph and Berta sat at a small table, close to the kitchen; a low lit candle dancing gently in the crosswind each time a waiter passed them by.

"Berta, I have something that I need to tell you," Joseph spoke to her across the table as they finished their meal. "Next week I'll have to fly back to America to take care of my grandmother. She's very ill and she needs me there with her." Thinking it sweet that he would fly half way across the world to care for his grandmother, Berta still could not squash down the selfish feeling of wishing he would stay. They had been spending a great deal of time together and the reality of him leaving broke her heart.

"When will you be coming back? That is, if you're coming back at all," Berta asked, her tone crafted to make him feel guilty even though she knew she had no right to make him feel that way.

"Of course I'll be coming back." he answered, "That's the other thing I wanted to talk with you about."

With that, Joseph rose from his seat, removed the napkin from his lap and placed it on the table. Moving to Berta he took her hand, lowering himself to one knee in front of her.

"Oh my...Joseph." Berta gasped, feeling the tears begin to sting her eyes.

"Now, before you say anything, I want you to know that the first thing I'd like to do when I get back is hire a lawyer and adopt Konnie. Although, it would make things much easier if you would first agree to marry me?" Berta had no hope of stopping the tears. She leapt from her chair, pulling Joseph up with her.

"Yes, yes, of course," she managed to squeak out, her throat choked with emotion. As they embraced, she knew that she had found what she had been searching for. She thought she could make a life with this man and her daughter.

The euphoric feeling of her engagement surrounded Berta like a warm blanket after that night. She was still floating on love's cloud when she spotted Joseph at a dance hall several weeks after he had supposedly left for America. She watched in disbelief as he danced with a strange woman. The moment he noticed her, Joseph immediately came to her to explain—he claimed he had gotten cold feet and begged for her forgiveness. She did finally decide to forgive him.

The next day they traveled from Bitburg to Trier where he bought her an engagement ring. On March 29th in 1961 they got married under German law; then, on April 4th of that same year, their union was declared in an American church on base.

Eventually they went back to Trier to formally adopt Konnie. Berta's Papa was not privy to the couple's plans for Konnie; she allowed him to believe he had total rights over the young girl.

Once the proceedings were complete, Joseph and Berta tried several times to have Konnie (now five) stay with them, but she loved her grandfather and wanted no part of living elsewhere.

Throughout the attempts to transition Konnie into their home, Berta discovered that she was expecting the newest member of the family. Baby Michael was welcomed on March 22, 1962.

Leaving for America

Joseph eventually received new orders stating they would be leaving for America soon. Berta finally informed Papa that she had full custody of Konnie and would be bringing her with them to the states. The old man shook as he cried, begging them to let her stay—he said that little Konnie was the only thing he had to live for. After much deliberation, Berta decided that staying with her grandfather was truly in Konnie's best interest. Regretfully, they left her in Germany and went back to America.

The orders were for Joseph to be stationed at Loring AFB in Maine. Of course once they arrived in the United States Joseph took Berta and Michael to meet his family in Auburn, Maine.

The entire family came running out of the camp to greet Joseph and did not acknowledge Berta or their baby. In a flurry of hugs and slaps on the back, Joseph was ushered inside—leaving Berta standing alone, outside, with Michael in her arms. Several minutes later, her father-in-law came out to greet her and escort them both inside.

Berta sat in silence as everyone around her enthusiastically engaged in conversation. Being that she didn't speak a word of French, Berta felt extremely isolated. She finally asked Joseph where she and Michael could go rest for a little while. He led her to a room and then returned to the commotion of his family. The next morning, Joseph had to go to the base to sign documents and left Berta there with his grandmother who spoke no English.

After waking up, Berta sat Michael in a high chair for his morning feeding. Joseph's Aunt, came into the kitchen and yelled at her in French because Berta had reprimanded Michael for not eating. After she was done, Berta began to clean all of the rooms in the camp. She swept and gathered a pile of dust and debris near Grandmother's chair. Then, she went into the bathroom to clean and when she came out a few minutes later she saw Grandmother messing up the pile of dirt with her newspaper.

After the confrontation with the Aunt and seeing what the Grandmother had done Berta had enough and said with a stern voice.

"You're a bitter old lady."

The grandmother then got up from her chair and hurried outside screaming, "Help me! She wants to kill me!"

Joseph had arrived at that moment and, appallingly, the first words out of his mouth were, "What have you done to my grandmother?" He told Berta to get their belongings together—that they would be leaving because he found an apartment and she couldn't be trusted with his grandmother.

They settled into their apartment. Life early on was a challenge. Berta could not do anything right in Joseph's eyes and Michael was continuously sick. Joseph seemed to work all the time—days doing his military duties and nights bar-tending at The Officer's Club—and Berta was extremely homesick. Joseph's family constantly harassed Berta—calling several times to accuse Michael of not being Joseph's baby and calling him a bastard. They called Berta a Nazi whore and offered her money to go back to Germany with her bastard child.

One night, in particular Joseph's grandmother had called to pressure Berta into going back home—claiming that her grandson did not even love her. Berta had begun to cry just as Joseph walked in from working his second job. He noticed his wife in tears and grabbed the phone away from her to listen to what his grandmother was saying. He was so alarmed by what he heard, he explained loudly, "Grandmother!...I never thought you would be involved in all this bullshit.". Berta went upstairs to try and comfort Michael who had a 105° fever at the time. Berta had enough of Joseph's family and all of their fighting.

On a day when the couple's fighting had gotten rather voluminous, the next door neighbor—Jean—suggested that Berta go see a lawyer on the military base to help her file for divorce and get back to Germany. Berta took her advice and sought council that day.

The next day, Berta received a phone call from the legal office saying that they wanted a meeting at the marital home at 1pm to sign legal documents. Joseph arrived at noon, begging Berta to stay.

"I love you...I don't want to lose you. Tell me what I can do to make our lives better." He pleaded; his cheeks stained by the steady flow of tears."

Berta said "The only way I will stay married to you is if you can get our family back to Germany." The attorney present informed Joseph he could make this request this to the Base Commander, understanding how important his family was to him, went immediately to see the Commander. Joseph was granted new orders, several months later, to be stationed at Bitburg Air Force Base in Germany.

New Orders

For almost three years the family prospered in Bitburg, Germany. There were many enjoyable times with peace amongst the family, and Michael was healthy and happy. Life was good.

In the summer of 1966 Joseph received new orders for MacDill Air Force Base in Tampa, Florida. Because things had been so much better between them, Joseph and Berta did not find the news disappointing at all; they looked forward to the adventure.

Several months after arriving in Tampa, Berta discovered she was pregnant with her third child. On October 4, 1967, she gave birth to Brian, her second son. Early on, Brian had a hard time falling asleep; Joseph would cradle him in his arms while walking around the home singing, "Catch a falling star and put it in your pocket…"

In the fall of 1968, Joseph received yet another new set of orders to be stationed in Thailand. He was required to make the trip alone due to the fact that his family was not allowed near a war zone. Joseph and Berta agreed that she would take the boys to live in Auburn, Maine to be closer to family—the same family that had mistreated her years earlier.

Berta and the boys settled into an apartment in Auburn shortly thereafter. A couple months later Joseph received word that his grandmother had passed away and left him the home on Taylor Pond. Joseph was not able to fly home for the funeral and gave power of attorney to Berta so she could expedite all of the paperwork and take possession of the home. Berta went to see the attorney who ended up being very rude and asked her if she was a Nazi or if her father was a Nazi. Berta was shocked and replied, "No I'm not a Nazi and neither is my Papa."

Later that same day, Berta received a call from the woman who lived next door to Grandmother's home. She told her about the cousins and other family members who were inside the home, removing many items. Berta called the police immediately and told them what was going on. She explained that she was the wife living alone and her husband was in the Air Force, stationed in Thailand.

The police reacted quickly and placed a seal on the door of the camp, warning everyone to keep out.

The next day, the police showed up at Berta's apartment to confirm ownership and power of attorney. Berta requested that the police escort her to the home and allow her access. They agreed. Shortly thereafter the police brought Berta and the boys to the camp and they were allowed to go inside.

Going inside for the first time was a shock and a disappointment. All of the furniture was missing and the bed in Grandmother's room was destroyed. Also many of the floor boards were lifted up—Grandmother was known for hiding money in the floor boards. Berta assumed that's what they were looking for and that they had probably found whatever money she had hidden. The home had clearly been ransacked and exactly as the neighbor had described.

Berta began the long and arduous task of cleaning the home; she scrubbed the walls and floors until all of the filth was removed. Berta was happy to be cleaning the two bedroom home; she knew the boys would appreciate their room and Berta wanted to make it comfortable for Joseph when he returned from duty.

After the camp was ready for the family to move in, Joseph's cousin, Richard—who was a mover by trade—was willing to help Berta and the boys from transition out of their apartment. Berta was grateful for Richard's assistance. Richard followed through with his promise and moved all of the families belongings into the home.

The home was located right on the lake. Berta and the boys enjoyed picnics nearby the local beach, as well as walking through the serene atmosphere of the neighborhood. Life was good for almost an entire year afterwards.

Then one night while Berta was watching television, she heard a noise on the porch outside. Frightened, she ran to her room to get a loaded .22 caliber pistol. When she came back out, she cautiously looked out the window.

She could see shadows of people and flames. Concerned, Berta swung open the door, pistol in hand, and startled to find a crowd of people singing 'Happy Birthday' to her—the flames were actually candles on a birthday cake. Berta recognized that the crowd of people were actually the cousins who had mistreated her when she first arrived in the United States. She demanded that they get off her property and warned that she did not want to see them again. That infuriated the crowd, and they began to shout hateful things to Berta. She pointed the gun at them and threatened to shoot them if they didn't get out of there. Because they believed Berta would honor her word, the crowd dispersed.

Berta went back inside and tried to calm down from the frightful event that evening—and that's when the phone rang. It was her Papa on the other line calling from Germany. He was extremely distraught, asking Berta to come and pick up Konnie because he could no longer handle her. Konnie was eleven years old at the time and very spoiled by her grandfather and uncles, who showered her with gifts and attention. Berta felt bad about the situation Konnie was in and told her Papa that she would have to speak with the Red Cross to get Joseph stationed in Germany again.

Berta reached out to the Red Cross the next day. They were very empathetic of her situation and asked where Joseph was currently stationed. The Red Cross was very helpful in contacting the Base Commander in Thailand and explaining the situation—requesting an immediate transfer for Joseph to Germany.

Within three weeks, Joseph received orders to be stationed in Haun AFB, Germany; however, he would fly to the United States first to collect Berta and the children.

Berta and her family arrived at Haun AFB in 1972. They drove immediately to Berta's Papa's house in Trier to retrieve Konnie. When they arrived, Konnie was ready and waiting with her belongings. After a brief conversation with her Papa, Berta and the children drove to their apartment in Rhaunen—only fifteen minutes away from where Joseph would be working.

The family was finally complete now; with Konnie and the two boys all living together. They shared a three bedroom apartment together for several years. During that time, Joseph assisted with the opening of a new Air Force base in Zweibrucken, Germany. Fortunately, the new base was close enough that Joseph could commute back and forth to his apartment.

Berta's Beginnings

Dream Come True

In 1975, Joseph received orders for Griffis AFB in Rome, New York. Berta's family packed up their belongings, flew to the United States and moved into a mobile home in Stoneybrook. The trailer park was wonderful: located close to where Joseph worked and where the kids went to school; beautiful, open fields to play in; and lush surroundings. Pine trees were scattered around the edges of the park, giving way to a dense forest brimming with nature—a small stream meandered through the center. The children's' schools were very close. The family enjoyed living there for about a year, until a home became available on base.

Berta and her family were no strangers to moving and quickly settled into their new home. It was during this time that Berta had the opportunity to reflect back on a childhood dream: being a beautician and salon owner. Wondering if it could ever come true, she discussed the possibility with Joseph.

Joseph came home early one weekday and surprised Berta, offering to take her to lunch. Knowing the kids were in school, she happily accepted.

"Where are we going?" Berta asked excitedly.

"I'm taking you to a restaurant in Utica." Joseph responded, eyes twinkling. Berta was unfamiliar with this city, but she was content to be spending time with her husband.

The couple arrived before a large storefront. "Let's go in and see what they have." Joseph said. At that precise moment, Berta noticed a large, glossy, black sign hanging in front. In boldly contrasted white letters, the sign read: Cosmetology School. Berta felt anxious and excited, simultaneously, as they stepped inside.

Joseph was filled with joy and smiling ear to ear at Berta's reaction. He escorted Berta inside to meet with the director—with whom he had already scheduled an appointment with several weeks earlier. The director of the school was very kind and showed the couple around the facility. Berta was impressed and knew she wanted to learn more. The director also mentioned that he offers rides to students living in the Rome area. Berta thought this was the perfect arrangement, seeing as Joseph needed the only car the family owned to get to and from work. Berta couldn't be happier to sign the papers; she would begin taking classes the following week.

The first week she spent at Cosmetology School was exhilarating for Berta. Her dream was now possible, and she entrenched herself in learning all that she could. The staff and director were impressed by her voracious desire to learn—challenging her early and often with new styles and techniques.

When class was over, Berta studied diligently at home while caring for her children and managing the household chores. Joseph was not home very often. He worked long hours and several jobs to provide for his family and give Berta the opportunity to make her dream come true.

The second week proved to be more challenging and even more rewarding. The director came over to Berta's station and asked her to serve the next customer in line.

Berta smiled and nodded. She was excited about the opportunity. This was her first customer.

    Berta was a bit nervous initially, but managed to keep her composure and greet the lady with a pleasant, professional smile. Confidently, she asked the woman back to her work station. After escorting the lady to her work station Berta asked if she knew what she wanted, or if she was looking for any suggestions. The lady was stylishly dressed and had an air of refinement about her. Speaking with a modicum of trepidation, she asked Berta what she would suggest. Berta described the newest style of the day and how it would look on her. The lady was willing, at this point, to try something new and trusted Berta to deliver an amazing hair style that would impress her friends at the social club. Berta accomplished exactly that. The woman was very pleased with the service she received and Berta was oblivious to the nod of approval from the director.

    A total of nine hundred hours—a combination of instruction and actually performing the techniques learned in class—were required for licensure. It was also mandatory that Berta write an essay and execute a styling procedure in front of the Cosmetology Board. After Berta had finished her final review, the evaluator instructed her to go home. Berta asked why she was being sent home, and the evaluator told Berta that she was a natural and she would be receiving her license in the mail within a few weeks. Realizing that her childhood dream has come true, Berta cried and hugged the evaluator. Berta thanked her and left with an immense joy in her heart. She couldn't wait to get home and share the news with her husband and children.

Elisabeth's Beauty Salon

In 1976, Joseph received emergency orders to travel alone to Kunsan, Korea. They thought it best to have Berta and the children move back to Maine to be closer to family. They packed up yet again and found a rental home in Auburn to live in. After they were all settled, Joseph left for Korea and served the better part of a year there before returning to Maine and his final duty station at Pease AFB, New Hampshire. Joseph served proudly in the United States Air Force for twenty-one years before his honorable retirement in August of 1977.

When Joseph returned from Korea, him and Berta decided to purchase their first home. They found the home they were looking for in Auburn and moved in right away. Months later, Berta was yearning to open her own salon. After discussing it with Joseph, they both agreed that they could open a salon out of the ground floor of their home—there was even a separate entrance; perfect for running a business.

They purchased furniture and equipment to make the salon comfortable and modern—with all the latest tools a hair stylist would need. Joseph, being skilled at carpentry, made Berta a beautiful sign to post out on the front lawn. The sign was made of wood and shaped elegantly, painted all in white. In large black lettering it read: Elisabeth's Beauty Salon, with a phone number appearing underneath. The only thing missing now were customers.

    Within the first week of opening her salon, a neighbor from across the street stopped in and asked Berta if she would cut her hair. After she finished, the neighbor was so impressed, she said she would tell all her friends what a fabulous stylist Berta was. Berta was grateful for the neighbor's kind words and referral. A few days later, Berta started receiving more phone calls from local ladies who wanted to schedule appointments. Business picked up rapidly, requiring Berta to work seven days a week. Women from all walks of life sat in Berta's chair. The Police Chief's wife, as well as the Mayor's wife, had their hair done by Berta. The business was incredibly profitable thanks to Berta's talent and charming personality.

The mailman stopped in one day and asked Berta if she cut men's hair. "Of course!" Berta replied. "Although, no men have made an appointment." The mailman would become her first male customer. After his haircut, he told Berta that he would refer all of the men and woman at the post office to her. Berta was delighted by the referral—further validation that she was living her dream.

Months went by, and Elisabeth's Beauty Salon was a success: business was fantastic, customers were happy, and the salon became a meeting place for all the ladies in town.

One day after closing her salon for the evening Berta, sitting in her own stylists' chair, reflected back over her life with a full heart and no regrets. She thought about how incredible it was to have survived the human savagery she had witnessed: watching her best friend's father shot in the head right in front of her; and surviving several bombing raids during World War II—that nearly destroyed the town she grew up in. She thought about; losing her beloved Mama at age nine and witnessing the decline of her Papa as a result of her death. That brought up memories of her horrible stepmother and the torment she endured—leading her to running away from her family and childhood home. Berta remembered being raped at age nineteen and acknowledged she was no longer angry about it anymore—she was so blessed to be able to watch her daughter grow into a beautiful and strong woman herself. Berta then contemplated what she missed during the month long coma she incredibly had woken up from. With a smile, she remembered the handsome gentlemen who had won her heart and given her two boys to love and be proud of.

Her life may not have been paved with the smoothest of stone, but it was a path that Berta felt privileged to walk. Looking around her salon one more time, she thanked her lucky stars and with a smile that felt permanently etched in her face, Berta went upstairs to kiss her beautiful family goodnight.

EPILOGUE

Elisabeth Berta Couture is a survivor, a mother, and a wife. The title of her story signifies the many opportunities she had to start over, overcome, and not succumb to the hardships, perilous situations, and bad people she encountered throughout her life.

Berta's hope is that her story might help someone discover their inner strength and persevere through any of life's difficult moments.

Made in the USA
Middletown, DE
25 May 2017